Synopsis

This book continues Ruth's memoir beginning with her first book "To Love, Honour and Betray". The book documents Ruth's experience in the depths of a terrible transatlantic situation when a Social Media scammer offers Ruth an 'amazing' business opportunity. He plays on her good nature and vulnerability and they become firm friends and after a while romance blossomed. Unbeknown to Ruth this man was a dangerous pathological liar. He was calculating and a serial scammer, stalking her profile for five months on social media and targeting her without conscience.

Eventually, after many conversations, the man convinced Ruth of a business opportunity based in America, all the while assuring her that her involvement would be based in London. He persuaded Ruth to fly to Nashville for a ten day fact finding visit. A terrifying ordeal ensues when Ruth's passport goes 'missing' the day before she is due to fly back home. This man slowly manipulated Ruth and drained Ruth's finances with constant promises that he would pay her back through the business. Ruth found herself trapped with him in Brooklyn for eight months, living in hope that she would get her money back. Surviving through his various scams and promises. During this time Ruth discovers his volatile and dangerous nature and becomes fearful of him. How does she get out of this terrible situation? How does she rebuild her life? How does she recover from such humiliation and shame?

This book is both a cautionary tale and beautifully written in Ruth's own words. It is a demonstration of how it is so easy to get sucked into a perilous situation when you trust someone. It proves how it is possible to get through anything with bravery, determination, strength, and the love of family and true friends. It is a sincere, honest letter to Ruth's earlier self and her adult children in which Ruth bravely shares her story so that others can find strength and inspiration.

Why do we overlook the "signs" and trust when we shouldn't? Do we want to believe that something good can come our way? That "now, finally, our dreams can come true"? In this part of the book Ruth was charmed, deceived, and manipulated into believing that she finally deserved a better life for her and her children. Was this opportunity finally her answer? Is this dangerous man still at large deceiving others on social media?

About the author...

Ruth Tunnicliffe is a loving mum to three adult children. Throughout her life experience she has grown from shy and submissive to becoming a strong survivor and now an independent thriver. By putting pen to paper her work of pure liberation will be sure to help and inspire other women who find themselves treading a similar path of enforced agreeability. A fault in society is that women are effectively conditioned to please others and not to speak up or complain.

Ruth's life is documented so beautifully in her books and demonstrates how 'putting up and shutting up' can result in making near impossible choices and heart-breaking decisions to protect others.

Ruth started writing in 2011, initially for cathartic reasons. After years of living with the guilt and sadness throughout her experiences, she felt that writing everything down would help her explain some of the tough decisions she had made to her children. Ruth separated from her two eldest children following the breakdown of her first marriage due to her ex-husband's violent and abusive behaviour.

Making the decision to leave her eldest son and daughter with their father was, without doubt, the most difficult selfless, and heart-breaking decision she would ever have to make. At the time Ruth was working fulltime as a legal secretary. Her children were primarily looked after by their father who was working part time. When the marriage ended, Ruth wanted to make sure that her children remained secure and in their home. Ruth did not want to uproot them from their school and time with their friends. So, she minimised any disruption to their routine.

Though extremely traumatised, Ruth had no doubt that by removing herself from the situation, she would be protecting her children and there would be no further threat of violence or abuse around them. She didn't want her children to watch while their father disrespected their mother, nor witness such unacceptable behaviour. Even though it was an extremely emotional and a hugely difficult decision for her, she hoped that her children would understand her reasons in time. She was sure that her ex-husband would never harm her children. Despite everything he was a good father. She had no doubt that he would continue to take loving care of them.

Ruth felt that she needed a clear 3 months to be able to finish writing. She struggled to find time to concentrate on it while she was working. During the first Covid-19 lockdown she found herself redundant, so continued writing. Once she started to write, the flood gates opened and she couldn't stop. She kept writing everyday and sent chapters to her friend at the end of the day for her to read. Every chapter she wrote helped to unravel her life. It was difficult to continue at times but with the encouragement from her friend, Ruth continued and finished after eight weeks.

In Ruth's life story a second marriage followed. Over time this man became increasingly paranoid, unpredictable, and dangerous. After constant pressure and coercive behaviour from him, Ruth reluctantly agreed to move to Cornwall to care for his aging father. This move took her further away from her eldest children.

The marriage ended years later when Ruth, her second son, and daughter, who was living with her by then, were forced to go into hiding when he began stalking them, behaving erratically and dangerously.

After both marriages ended Ruth set about cheerfully building back her life. Always optimistic and managing to keep her sense of fun and humour, she faced prejudice from friends and acquaintances who thought they would have done things differently.

But what Ruth's story shows is that these experiences can, and do, happen so naturally. That before you know it, you are in a perilous situation. There is also humour in Ruth's writing and she is not afraid to laugh at herself.

This real-life story is a page-turner. It is a book you will read in one on two sittings. You will not want to put it down. Written as Ruth speaks, it is like sitting down with a friend as they tell you the best *'real life'* stories ever. It has served as a very cathartic and healing process for Ruth. She has been through so much and rebuilt her life more times than most people ever have to.

Acknowledgements

Massive thanks go to my dear friend Sunny Chayes for her love and support throughout this difficult journey. Her endless patience and support carried me through a very arduous edit.

I also wish to thank my amazing husband Richard, for his love, understanding and patience. Writing the book has been all consuming and without Richard's support I may have given up.

Thanks also go to my publisher, Chris Day for believing in me, for his advice and care and of course my Agent, Susan Mears, for her continuing love and support.

Dedication

In Memory of my devoted Mother and Father.

My much loved Brother and Sister.

My precious and adored children.

To my wonderful husband, Richard. You have my heart.

Swindled, Stranded & Survived

by Ruth Tunnicliffe
© 2022

Published by
Filament Publishing Ltd
16, Croydon Road, Beddington
Croydon, Surrey CR0 4PA
www.filamentpublishing.com
+44(0)20 8688 2598

Swindled, Stranded & Survived
Ruth Tunnicliffe
ISBN 978-1-915465-00-9
© 2022 Ruth Tunnicliffe

The right of Ruth Tunnicliffe to be recognised
as the author of this work has been asserted by
her in accordance with the Designs and Copyrights
Act 1988 Section 77

All rights reserved
No portion of this work may be copied in any
way without the prior written permission
of the publishers

Printed in the UK

Table of Contents

PART ONE - THINGS CAN ONLY GET BETTER   13

CHAPTER 1 - What's the Story?   14

CHAPTER 2 - A Life Changing Call 2005   20

CHAPTER 3 - Sweet Brutus 2009   38

CHAPTER 4 - Suspicion Rising 2010   54

CHAPTER 5 - Two Hours To Leave 2010   62

CHAPTER 6 - It's Over 2010   77

CHAPTER 7 - Losing Owen   90

PART TWO - THE AMERICAN DREAM   99

CHAPTER 8 - Curiosity & Temptation 2011   100

CHAPTER 9 - Hello Fraser 2011   111

CHAPTER 10 - Trust Me Baby 2011   129

CHAPTER 11 - Hope & Promises   139

CHAPTER 12 - Spinning Yarns   145

CHAPTER 13 - Expensive Perfume & Designer Shades   153

CHAPTER 14 - My Ticket Back to Reality   158

CHAPTER 15 - Six Weeks to Turn it Around   173

PART THREE - PICKING UP THE PIECES   193

CHAPTER 16 - Sweet Tea & Seagulls   194

CHAPTER 17 - Full Circle   202

CHAPTER 18 - Genuine Solid People   212

CHAPTER 19 - The Life Changing Party   231

CHAPTER 20 - The Interview   238

CHAPTER 21 - Happily Ever After? 2013   252

EPILOGUE   264

PART ONE
THINGS CAN ONLY GET BETTER

CHAPTER 1

What's the Story?

Hi, my new reader friend. My name is Ruth and this is my humble and cautionary story. What a story it is! I decided that writing this would be my only hope in hell to make sense of it all for myself. So, thank you in advance for your patient indulgence. I will do my absolute best to make this crazy tale, amusing. So, settle down with your cup of tea, or something stronger and here we go with a northern country mum's accounting of my life so far; now reaching my half century mark.

I was born in the swinging sixties. Although there wasn't so much swinging in my northern small village, or at least to childhood eyes. During my childhood I lived modestly in a small village with my loving Mam, Dad, and older siblings Harry and Dina. The village was surrounded by beautiful countryside and I have many fond memories of our time there. Dad worked very hard as a milkman. He was a passionate farmer at heart having been brought up on his uncle's farm. Mam was a warm and wonderful homemaker. She would spend many hours knitting colourful themed jumpers on her huge loom that lived in the middle of our living room. She knitted hats, scarves, and gloves with her knitting needles for the family. She also baked gorgeous cakes and other delights on Sundays that we enjoyed and shared with family, friends, for church events. I spent most of my childhood days playing with my best friend Lizzie. She lived on a farm close by with her mam, dad, and brother Rex. I felt loved, safe, and very happy in those days.

I was eleven when Dad took a job as Farm Manager at an Equestrian Centre in Hackness. So, we moved away from our family and friends to begin our new life there. This was when I discovered my love for horses. I spent most of my teenage years working at the Equestrian Centre. Instead of payment I was given free riding lessons once a week. Luckily, I was able to ride every day after school and on weekends. I adored being with the horses and became a very accomplished rider. I entered competitions and won quite a few rosettes.

Even though I was a shy teenager, I made some amazing friends at the stables. We were a team. We all worked together and had a tremendous bond. There was nothing like the early morning dew dripping off the stable doors or the warm breath of the horses as we hacked along the roads and the huge English breakfast, we all enjoyed together afterwards. Nothing beats the feeling of being on an event horse. Flying over the fences on the back of such a magnificent animal, landing safely and galloping on to the next jump. I loved to prance around the dressage ring with grace. We felt such camaraderie on the show days cheering each other on and celebrating each of our wins. I believe my first love was with my friend's dapple grey gelding Gorgeous Grey. He will stay in my heart for ever. I'll never forget laying down with him in his stable at the end of a long ride.

I stepped out of my world and into a place where I was important, it was like a fantasy world where I could escape. Having the connection with the horse world gave me so much confidence and I really felt part of something special. It was an important time in my teenage development to becoming a young lady. I felt like I belonged and my contribution to this world was significant. I'm not sure I have ever felt like that since those wonderful days.

When I left school, it was obvious that I really wanted a career with horses. I loved that world so much, it was my special world and I knew I was accomplished enough. Without financial backing sadly that was not to be. My riding days and my life with the horse world came to an end when we moved away from the Equestrian Centre. Dad changed his job and so we moved further into the town. So, I decided to go to secretarial college. I did a two year secretarial course where I enjoyed new friendships and learned the trade.

After I completed the course, I took a training job as a dental nurse. This was where I met my first husband, Donovan. He came to the dentist for a regular check up and soon after we began dating. He was intriguing, a dark horse, mysterious and handsome. I fell for him very quickly and was overwhelmed with joy when he appeared to fall for me too. Donovan was a loner; a complex character. I wanted to make him happy; as is my usual way. He could be opinionated and firm at times but I believed that he was a lost soul and just needed love. I wanted more than anything to give him that love and to take care of him. We moved in together after about a year of dating. A year later we got engaged and naturally marriage followed. It just felt right, but I was later to learn that it was so wrong. I loved Donovan with all my heart. He definitely loved me too.

After a couple of happy years together, we had our first child, Tyler. We were both elated to welcome our son into the world. Donovan had been adopted when he was a baby, so he had always yearned for a child of his own. After Tyler's birth Donovan became more argumentative and opinionated. I could feel myself becoming submissive and was beginning to feel unable to speak out or voice my opinions at times. I just wanted to make Donovan happy and look after our son, Tyler. We continued along life's path. When Tyler was a toddler, I became pregnant with our daughter, Sarah. We had our lovely little family unit. At that time, I thought that we were complete. Little did I know there would be another little one in the future.

Heart break followed for me when Donovan became increasingly physically violent towards me. So, I painfully removed myself from the marriage. At that time, I felt that Donovan was a devoted and caring dad to Tyler and Sarah but dangerous towards me. His violence grew to such a stage that I feared for my life. He was out of control towards me. When he screamed at me, "I hope you die in your sleep," or worse… unmentionable, I absolutely believed that at some stage he would kill me. I feared that he would follow through with his threats. I feel like the violent abuse that I suffered would end tragically.

The one thing about Donovan was that he was a devoted father. The kids were his whole world and all he ever wanted. It was so clear to me that their wellbeing was paramount to him. I had absolutely no doubt that Donovan would take great care of them both. It never entered my mind that he would be anything less than a loving and responsible dad because they were everything to him. I felt so strongly that he would do everything in his power to keep them safe, happy, and well raised. I was sure that my kids would be fathered well. As the violence was directed at me, I felt that by removing myself from Donovan all would be well for my kids. I felt that I was the problem.

Argh mental block...

… ok I'm sipping tea. It's not helping.

As I'm trying to write the next part of my life, I'm boring myself; and I promised you I'd be amusing. So, perhaps you'll read my first book, To Love Honour and Betray. It's all there. It was painful enough the first time for me to write it. I don't know if I can bear the process a second time. So, give it a go. Perhaps you will find bits of yourself in the first chapters of my life. I am told that it is an interesting ride and a very relatable story.

Now that your pretty well caught up, lets get rolling……

CHAPTER 2

A Life Changing Call - 2005

I met and married my second husband Paul within three years. He was ex-forces, tough and a charismatic bloke. After eighteen months, my gorgeous boy Owen was born. A year or so later we moved to Somerset and into the house of Paul's ailing father. During this time, my lovely dad passed away. A month later Angus passed as well and Paul inherited the house so we officially moved in.

After living her best life for the summer in Greece teenage Sarah joined us in Somerset. She loved her time on the island with her boyfriend Jason and his lively Greek family. They all enjoyed fun in the sun and breaking plates after eating the amazing traditional food. Jason and Sarah whizzed around on their bikes on cobblestone streets in the sun with their many friends. The whole experience certainly suited her; she absolutely blossomed. Now that she was back, she spent most of her time at the farm and helping Jason's mother Anna at the family café in town. Happily, she managed to squeeze in a visit to see us now and again.

Tyler had been very musical since he was a toddler. He continued drumming throughout High School where he became the drummer in his first metal band. They all met in school and they started doing gigs around the local pubs. At this stage Tyler was living with his dad in Hackness. His health challenges that started when he was around nine, continued. Somehow, he was able to balance his health issues with the many hours of band practises and the late night gigs. He was so dedicated to the music. It seemed like it just fed his soul. Ever since he was a little boy he drummed and tapped on everything near him; to the point that the teachers at school gave him bongos to occupy him. Maybe this constant drumming would drive some mums mad but I always felt and heard the music in him. I recognised in him that his heart and soul were in that drumming. From such a young age I could feel the music coming from inside of him and bursting through. This might sound odd but it felt like his heart was drumming on the outside.

Back at the house, Paul was spending his inheritance from his father. He was shopping like a lottery winner; it was his money so I didn't have a say in it. We were mortgage free, so Paul seemed to have the attitude of 'Que Será, Será,' whatever will be will be. He was spending money on all kinds of car parts. He was constantly looking for Minis to restore. He found and bought a limited edition sparkly forest green Mazda MX5. It was a two-seater soft top. He told me that I could use it as my car.

He wanted his 'trophy wife' swanning around in a sparkly sports car. The trouble was that Owen had to spend most of his time squashed beside Sarah sharing a seatbelt. Luckily, the two of them found that hilarious.

I secured a new job as Personal Assistant to the Registrar at the local university. He was called Philip. What a great guy. He was ridiculously small. He got his suits from the child section of the exclusive department store Marks and Spencer. We got on amazingly well as soon as we met. He was witty, clever, and very charming. We bounced off each other and worked well together. I really liked him. Mrs Driver, the Clairvoyant I had seen in Hackness years before, had been right. I had indeed gone higher in my profession as she predicted; eerie! I felt like I was doing something meaningful. I was now a Personal Assistant.

I loved the job. Even though the work was challenging and important, there were fun moments too. Like watching the comical Philip gliding around his office practising his quirky ballroom moves. He and his wife attended ballroom classes twice a week. He mentioned that he wanted to be better than her so hence the lunchtime dancing. We were constantly laughing at each other's jokes. After a while, Paul started showing signs of jealousy. Once again, it was typical of him to feel insecure when I was working with a man that I got on well with. Even to the point that as soon as I got the job offer, Paul was showing signs that he didn't want me to take the job. Instead of being happy for me, the first thing he asked me about was my boss. I didn't even know him well at that point. Only that he had a cracking sense of humour and that we got on well. Paul had made himself known to everybody when I was at my last job; and not in a good way. I didn't want that to happen again. I wanted this to be a clean slate. What was Paul going to do next with a university full of new people for me to engage with?

He began to get suspicious every time I referred to anybody at work. I believed it was more 'natural' if I mentioned people at work. Which is why I told him about my co-workers, to put his mind at rest. I wanted to assure him that I wasn't going to disappear off into the sunset with somebody from work. This didn't seem to work because he would ring me and leave endless messages. I would occasionally pick up and he would try to keep me on the phone. The strange thing about it was that he would hardly speak to me while we were at home. He became relentless in calling me about every hour of the working day; obviously control issues. Occasionally, he even turned up without warning during the day, as if he was trying to catch me out. The man knew no boundaries.

I used to run for three miles along the

seafront during my lunch breaks. The sea was stunning and the exercise was exhilarating for me. I always felt euphoric and so healthy and refreshed. I was so blessed to have such a great reset in the middle of my day. I ran in all the various English weather; rain or shine. I felt extremely lucky to have such an amazing job and so near to the beach, too; I loved it. However, sometimes an angry Paul would be blocking my office door when I ran back. He didn't even use any pretence; he just told me that he was checking up on me. I really didn't want him to screw this up for me as he had in the past. Paul's constant disruptions weren't fair to me, to my co-workers, or my boss. We were all paid to do our jobs, not to be constantly interrupted and harangued by Paul!

Contact with Tyler during this time had become very sporadic. My feeling was that he was very loyal to my ex, Donovan. He often worried about leaving his dad for too long on his own. It was unfortunate how much effect Donovan had on Tyler. Donovan was supposed to be the parent, though it felt the other way around. In addition to the dad situation, Tyler had many friends in Hackness as well as his band practise and gigs with his best mates. He would also take the time to come down to Somerset and visit us now and again. Never enough for a mum, though.

Tyler and Owen got on very well. Owen loved

spending time with his big brother. Tyler would mess around with Owen's hair, styling it to look like a wig. It was good to see Tyler laughing. His face lit up when he laughed. I wished he did it more often. They would play on Xbox and go swimming together at the local community hotel pool. Tyler used to chuck Owen in the pool and watch him scramble to the surface. Tyler didn't have a lot of energy to swim in those days, though he loved messing around in the water with Owen. They loved swimming under the fountains. Sometimes, they would go to the beach with their body boards and surf.

The Alport's Syndrome which Tyler was diagnosed with when he was younger was now clearly affecting him. Donovan had told me that he was receiving regular health checks and his kidneys were being monitored. So, I believed him. I really wanted Tyler to stay with us longer, though he was very worried about his dad and would go back after a few days. It was extremely rare for all the kids to spend time together. When they did, it was Heaven for me.

Tyler was working on the fish counter in a local supermarket, temporarily. He really didn't know what he wanted to do next but most probably something in music. He didn't feel at that time that this band would be his career. The band was very popular but they weren't getting paid gigs yet. It was hard for him getting through each day with his kidney challenges. God knows how he mustered up the energy to work and practise with the band as well as gigs. He used to walk to work and back to save money. It was quite a trek, but he did it.

At that time, Tyler was increasingly concerned about his dad. He told me that he would often come home to find the oven on with nothing in it. There would be candles burning, with Donovan had passed out on the sofa. He was clearly not capable of keeping a safe home for Tyler. At this point, I tried to persuade Tyler to come and live with us. He was still insisting on staying with his dad; even though I felt like I should step in as his mother and have him live with me.

After a while sadly, Sarah and Jason the Greek split up. I assumed that it was a matter of them growing apart. The logical next step was for Sarah to come and live with us fulltime. It was coming up to Christmas so Tyler was also with us. I was over the moon to have all of my kids together. On Christmas morning, we all took a drive along the coast in our newly inherited Armstrong Sidley Sapphire car. What fun we had together that day.

After a few weeks, Sarah left Jason's mum's café and took a job at a local hotel, as a receptionist. She settled in quite nicely and soon met her next beau, Simon. He was a personal trainer at the gym in the hotel. They were good together, so after a while they decided to set up 'home.' They would come round for lunch on a Sunday, snuggle up and watch television and sometimes I'd catch them play wrestling in the afternoon. It was lovely to see Sarah so happy. They bought a dog called Brutus. He was a stocky little chug and darted around the house constantly. When they brought him to meet us, Brutus barked ferociously at Paul and bit him when he tried to stroke him. Sarah laughed and whispered to me, "He knows." Paul didn't want much contact with Brutus after that. He thought the dog was bonkers. Sarah and Simon treated Brutus like their child. They would dress him in little trousers and tops!

While Tyler had been with us over Christmas, I could tell that he wasn't feeling well, though I had no idea how compromised he actually was. He had managed to hide that from me very well. It was a Friday morning when I got a call from Tyler's kidney specialist. He told me that Tyler had asked him to call me. He had been at work in the supermarket when he began to feel really unwell. He knew that this was serious so he had decided to take himself to hospital. Thank God, he did. I had absolutely no idea that things were as bad as this. He said that he felt like everything was shutting down. The doctor told me that Tyler's kidneys were failing quickly and that he would immediately need to start dialysis. What? Dialysis for my son? How had it come to this, and how did I not know?

The doctor's diagnosis was that Tyler would need a transplant by the time he was in his early twenties. His kidneys had deteriorated quicker than had been expected. What? How on earth has this happened? I'm not sure why Tyler kept this to himself, but he did. He had missed a few appointments along the way. He had not been getting the medication he needed to keep his kidneys stable. The doctor insisted that Tyler receive proper care when he came out of hospital, so Tyler asked the doctor to ring me as he felt 'alone' and that I had always 'supported him.' Tyler was a very proud and private young man. It was clear that he wanted to take responsibility for this himself but it had all become too much. His illness had escalated so quickly that it surprised the doctors and got the better of Tyler.

Of course, I wanted Tyler with me, where I could take care of him. The doctor told me that Tyler would need a fistula in his wrist before he could start dialysis. I didn't know what a fistula was, so I asked the doctor to explain. He told me that it was a fusion of the veins in his arm, creating one big vein which they would use for the dialysis needle. I could not comprehend that Tyler's kidneys had deteriorated so. Almost immediately after the call, we drove the seven hour journey to see Tyler at hospital. We arrived first thing the next morning. I was shocked to see that he was as white as a sheet and didn't seem to have any life left in him. I wished to God that I could have swapped places with him. Looking back, it was heartbreaking that he didn't have the energy to race around or play football with his mates as a youngster. I felt that he had missed out on all of that. It goes without saying that at this stage I would do all I can to help him.

After a few days he started dialysis and his kidneys stabilised. At which point we drove back to Somerset. After a couple of weeks, Tyler was feeling better so he flew down to stay with us. He took Owen's bedroom and Owen moved into the smaller room. I felt extremely relieved to have him with us. The doctor transferred all of his records from Hackness and arranged for Tyler's care to be moved to Wells Hospital nearby. He needed to go for dialysis three times a week. Tyler was resigned to it, even though he hated it. I was amazed at how strong he was. On his treatment days, an ambulance car would pick him up from the house. It broke my heart to watch him walk to the ambulance.

Each day that he returned from treatment I would be at the door waiting with a snack for him. Nine times out of ten, he was too bushed to eat, he just didn't have an appetite and no interest in food. The treatment took its toll on him. He really missed his friends and his band mates in Hackness. During this time, his drumming was on hold. Now and again, he would go back to see them. We arranged for him to have what they called a 'dialysis holiday.' They would arrange for the treatment to be done in Hackness for the time that Tyler was staying there. He became well known to hospitals in Hackness and Wells. It was such an awful time for him and this went on for months. The doctor said that Tyler had been put on the list for a kidney transplant. As soon as we could, the whole family got assessed to see if any of us were suitable to donate a kidney to him. Sadly, we were told that Tyler had a rare blood group which meant that none of us could donate to him. He couldn't seem to catch a break. Any one of us would have given him one of our kidneys, without hesitation. Unfortunately, none of us could. It was awful to feel so helpless. We all felt like we were letting him down.

Tyler had been thinking about doing an art course at college. He was very artistic and creative. He would sketch cartoon characters. I thought they were fantastic so I encouraged him. I made enquiries at Wells College about a foundation course and he managed to get a place there. The course worked well with his dialysis days and allowed him to explore another creative path. Even though he found it quite hard juggling his studies with the dialysis treatments, he was determined to do well in his studies and get to university. I was so proud of him for all of this.

Tyler was getting really fed up with his trips to Wells. Even though we had been told that Tyler had been put on the national list for a transplant, he was beginning to give up hope. He kept saying that he was never going to get a kidney and that it was hopeless. I would tell him to keep positive and that he would definitely get the call. I had to believe this. There was no choice; it had to happen. The only way to get through this was to keep Tyler as well as myself upbeat and positive about it all.

Tyler suggested that he was thinking of not going for any more dialysis. I knew that he had reached the point where he just didn't care anymore. I was so worried that Tyler was going to give up. The consequences would be fatal. Other than taking him myself and sitting with him, there was nothing I could do to get him to go. But maybe there was something else I could do. So, I called the transplant administrator to check Tyler's position on the transplant list. When they checked the list, they discovered that his name was not on it. What? I was speechless, not to mention furious. They said that there must have been an oversight. An oversight?! No, this could not be true. Who dropped the ball? How in the world did this happen? I was so angry! I demanded that they rectify it, right then and there. I told them to confirm with me that he would be added to the list for Shepton Hospital, immediately. They explained to me that when

Tyler moved down to Somerset, he had been removed from the Hackness Hospital's waiting list and his name had not been added to the Shepton Hospital's list. They confirmed that he was now on the National list.

Actually, sometimes there is a silver lining. The fact that I checked Tyler's position on the list and found that he wasn't even on it, meant that the oversight was discovered. Now he was going to be added to the more expanded National list, where he had a far better chance of getting a kidney donation. Thank God for silver linings. The waiting game had begun, again.

Meanwhile, Tyler became much more positive knowing that he was on the National list. So, he began to consider going back to Hackness. He told me that he wanted to apply for a place at the university of fine art in Leathley. I was really pleased, even though I felt genuinely concerned about his health condition. How would he cope? Tyler needed to be looked after, I knew damn well that Donovan couldn't do it.

So, Tyler felt encouraged as he went off to university. After a couple of days, he rang me for a chat. He mentioned that he had met a bloke who lived a couple of doors away from him, called Kai. He said that Kai had invited Tyler round for a meal and they had an incredible time. It turned out that a life changing friendship between Tyler and Kai had begun. After a while, they formed a band with Kai as the singer, Gray on base, Graham on keyboard, and of course Tyler on the drums. They started performing for their friends in Kai's large lounge in his student house. They became extremely popular with the university students and started playing at university. He loved it and was becoming an incredibly talented musician.

Tyler succeeded in getting through the first year. I was delighted when he decided that he would come back to Somerset for the summer holidays. I couldn't wait to have him back with us. So, I immediately arranged for the dialysis to be transferred to Wells Hospital. They were all pleased to see Tyler back, too.

It was July and about 4:30 am when the phone rang. It was Shepton Hospital. A gentle female voice told me that they may have a kidney for Tyler. My heart missed a ton of beats. I went hot, then cold. I was excited, scared, and relieved all at the same time. My voice broke but I managed to ask them what we should do. Firstly, they told me to stay calm. Impossible! Next, they told me to take him to Shepton Hospital immediately. I was speechless, I couldn't believe it. This was what we had all being praying for. I felt like we had won the lottery! I went straightaway to wake Tyler, trying to keep my composure. Again impossible! I told him that we needed to take him to Shepton Hospital, "right now"! I explained that they may have a suitable kidney for him! He looked right at me, took a huge breath to compose himself and then calmly got out of bed. I packed a bag for him, then I woke Owen and we all jumped in the car. The sun was coming up as we drove from the house with the bright orange sunrise behind us. It felt like a good omen. We were all silent and with our own thoughts. Paul, for once, was quiet while he drove us to hospital. While we were on the way, I rang Sarah. Trying not to cry I said, "They have a kidney for Tyler! We are racing to hospital right now." Sarah blurted out, "Fuck, fuck, fuck." She asked if she should come, too. She kept repeating that she couldn't believe it. "Finally!" She was crying by the end of our call.

Tyler was so calm. He was amazing and seemed to be taking it all in his stride. This could be life changing for him. When we arrived at hospital a medical team was waiting for us. They worked together like clockwork. Once Tyler was settled into bed, they took several blood tests. They kept sweeping in and out of the room. They were on a mission. They didn't stop long enough to talk to any of us, yet I had so many questions. They seemed to know exactly what they were doing. We were all holding our breath waiting to hear whether the kidney was a suitable match for Tyler.

A couple of long hours later, Sarah burst through the door with Simon. I was so pleased to see them, as was Tyler. At that point, we still didn't know if the kidney would be a match.

Then at about 11:00 am, the doctor came in. I immediately asked him whether the kidney was a match. He casually replied, "Oh, yes, it is," as if we were supposed to know. He told us that they were ready to prepare Tyler for surgery. My heart burst. We all looked at each other in amazement. Sarah burst into tears and Simon had tears in his eyes, too. None of us could hardly believe it. Cool as ever, Tyler looked at me, and said, "Fair enough."

Tyler didn't seem scared or worried. He was unbelievably calm. Paul took Owen into town to get something to eat and told me that they would come back later. I fell into a trance, I just couldn't take all of this in. Sarah gave Tyler a hug. Simon shook Tyler's hand and wished him luck. We were told that the operation would take several hours. Sarah said that she couldn't stay that long. So, I promised them that I would ring Sarah as soon as Tyler was out of the operation. There was no way I was going to leave that hospital. The medical team came to take Tyler to the pre op room. They allowed me to walk beside him. It seemed like the longest walk, ever. I was shaking and so scared for Tyler. They stopped me at the pre op room door and told me that I couldn't go any further. I looked at Tyler, gave him a hug and wished him luck. I smiled at him and said, "This is it. This is the start of your new life, Tyler."

He smiled back at me as they wheeled him

into the surgery theatre. I cried as I sat outside the room. I didn't dare move, or even breathe, until I saw my Tyler again. I stayed outside the operating room for six hours in a complete daze. I didn't want to miss him coming round. The nurses had told me that there was a bedroom I could use if I wanted to stay the night. I didn't want to move, never mind leave hospital, so Paul took Owen home and I stayed. I promised that I would call when I had any news.

It must have been about 8:00 pm, when the nurses told me that Tyler was now in recovery. I was over the moon and couldn't wait to see him. He was very drowsy and glanced at me, smiled, then fell straight back to sleep. Thank God he was okay. He had survived the operation. I was beyond relieved. I could breathe again, finally. They suggested that I leave him for a while to recover. So, I went back to the little hospital bedroom. The nurses assured me that they would come for me as soon as I could see Tyler. After about four hours the nurse came to accompany me to Tyler's room. By that time, he had been moved to a ward. When I got there, I found him sitting upright, with a beaming smile on his face. I noticed that he had colour in his face and his skin looked smooth and moist. The whites of his eyes were bright. He looked so happy. He had a large jug of water next to him. He looked at me and with great delight, announced that he was allowed to drink as much as he wanted. This was such a gift for him. It was utterly amazing. He was incredibly happy. My heart burst with love to see him like that. I was so proud of him and what he had been through. It was as if someone had switched a light on in his soul. Tyler had been born again.

CHAPTER 3

Sweet Brutus 2009

The sweet omen of the previous day's golden sunrise came true as the next day was a beautiful sunny one as well. When I walked into Tyler's room the next morning, again, I found him sitting up in bed with a broad smile. He looked like a different person. I could see that life was flowing back through him. He was holding a jug of water up like a trophy, announcing "Look mum, I can drink!" To see that joy in his face was amazing. It was great for him now to be told that he could drink as much water as he wanted. It was an absolute gift. He was guzzling the jug of water, grinning from ear to ear.

When the consultant came in to see how Tyler was doing, he told us that the kidney started working immediately. It was a good match and was an extremely healthy kidney. Tyler should have no problems with it at all. When the consultant left the room, I followed him and stopped him in the corridor. He was such a quiet and unassuming man. I expressed my gratitude to him. I told him that I couldn't thank him enough for selecting Tyler for the transplant. I explained to him that Tyler was beginning to give up. This man had saved my son's life in so many ways. He was almost embarrassed as he told me that there was absolutely no need to thank him. He explained that when he noticed Tyler's name on the list, and his age, he thought that there was no doubt that Tyler should be given this chance. I shook his hand and thanked him once again on behalf of all of us. The doctor held my hand in both of his and nodded quietly. He seemed teary when he turned to walk away. What a hero. I will never forget him.

None of us dared to ask about the donor. It did not seem appropriate, even though we were all naturally curious as to where the kidney had come from. We were all more than aware that there was a family out there grieving. We honoured them and were sending prayers to them. We weren't told any specific details. I desperately wanted to thank the donor's family. I asked the hospital staff if it would be possible for us to do something to recognise what they had done for us. They said that we couldn't make direct contact with them, which I absolutely understood, but we could write to them. So, I wrote the family a letter from my heart, perhaps from one mum to another. I gave it to the consultant to pass on to them. We never heard back from them, although we have them in our prayers every day.

Tyler continued to improve by the hour. In no time at all, he was up and about; strolling up and down the ward. He remained in hospital for ten days to avoid infection and for monitoring the kidney for any signs of rejection. Though that was worrying, thankfully there were no signs of rejection right from the start. I visited Tyler every afternoon. My incredibly understanding boss, Philip gave me permission to come and go as I pleased. He was delighted for Tyler and for all of us.

I worked the mornings and then I caught the train to see Tyler. I simply had to see him every day. After ten days we brought Tyler home. He was getting stronger by the day and his appetite improved enormously. He couldn't stop eating! It was amazing for me watching him tucking in and having such an enormous appetite. He started to gain weight. He was so much happier. He was receiving excellent medical care with regular health checks and all the proper medications. At last, my Tyler could live a normal life. He could do anything he wanted to do. The world was now his oyster. The timing of this operation couldn't have been better. He stayed with us for the rest of that summer. He had a wonderful time spending hours on the beach with Owen. Even though Tyler had to be careful of his stitches, they made the best of their time together. They became buddies and were inseparable.

Tyler was due to go back to university late that September. The university gave him an extension, until he felt well enough to go back.

In October Tyler flew back to university. This would be his final year there. Naturally, I was very worried about him. He assured me that he would be fine. He told me that he would take care of himself and that he couldn't wait to start his new life. The band was doing well. They were performing more regularly at Kai's house, the university, and pubs around Leathley. They were becoming immensely popular. Tyler was loving it and he was doing well at university, too.

Tyler graduated from university the following July. Because we could only have four tickets, Owen and I went to his graduation. I wouldn't have missed it for the world. Sarah was disappointed that we couldn't have five tickets so that she could join us. We stayed with my beautiful bohemian friend, Evangeline who lived nearby. Tyler's dad Donovan had the third ticket and Tyler's lovely girlfriend, Minnie had the fourth. She was a lovely soul and incredibly sweet. I could tell that she adored Tyler. By this time, they were living together. Minnie had been looking after Tyler with love. Minnie was also studying at the university and had a part time job there, too. It all seemed to be working out well for them both.

When Tyler walked onto the stage to receive his scroll, by far, was one of the best moments of my life. He stood tall and glanced up at us as he raised his scroll in the air. What an achievement! I will never forget that feeling. Proud didn't come close. Minnie, Owen, and I were all jumping around. We were whooping for England, and Tyler. Tyler caught a glimpse of us all jumping around and smiled shyly as he left the stage. What an achievement! We celebrated over lunch after the ceremony. Then Owen and I drove back to Somerset with disco music and massive smiles all the way.

When we got home, it was back to reality with a bump for me. Paul began to act even more strangely. He was becoming extremely agitated as his paranoia grew. One day that week Paul told me that he was standing in a queue at the bakery, when he thought a man in the queue was saying derogatory things about him. Without a second thought, Paul grabbed the man, punched him in the face and knocked him against the counter. He then dragged him outside onto the pavement. Paul continued to punch the man, who now had a split lip and tongue. The woman behind the counter was shocked and called the police. The man under attack by Paul had run away by the time the police got there. Before the police arrived, Paul had convinced the woman behind the counter to vouch for him. She told the police that it was not Paul's fault. She must have been terrified. Paul was not charged. When Paul told me the story, he told it as a victory. I was speechless. This behaviour was not acceptable, and scary.

I began to think that I was in danger. Paul was clearly becoming even more unhinged.

Paul was often caught spying on Sarah. He would turn up unexpectedly while she was out shopping, and then follow her. Sarah often called me while he was behind her. She asked me to stay on the phone until he was gone. I told Paul many times that he had to stop such bizarre behaviour towards Sarah. He would shrug his shoulders and say that we were both overreacting. He told me that he was keeping an eye on her, nothing more. Owen was also becoming aware of his dad's erratic behaviour. He kept asking me what was wrong with him. I told Owen that his dad had a few issues but that he shouldn't worry. I tried to reassure him. I constantly talked to Paul about his paranoia and this erratic behaviour. But every time we spoke about it, he would insist that there was nothing wrong with him. He said that it was everyone else with the problem. It was clear to me that Paul was in denial. I tried my best to persuade him to get some professional help. He flatly refused. Instead, he would get angry and end up stomping out of the house. I felt that I was fighting a losing battle.

One day, unexpectedly, Sarah called me while she was working at the hotel. She was in a terrible state. When I eventually managed to calm her down, she told me that she and Simon had split up. I asked her what on earth had happened. She was too upset to tell me. I told her that I was on my way, immediately. When I arrived, Sarah was in the back office, crying. I gave her a hug. She began sobbing. This broke my heart. I felt so sad for her. I wished that it was me, and not her going through all this pain. I couldn't bear to see my girl this hurt and upset.

Sarah arranged a free room for her to stay in at the hotel. She didn't want to come back home with me. She didn't want to explain anything to Paul. She felt that he would make a meal of it, and that would make things even worse. She needed some time to think it all through. Sarah had already decided that she would stay at the hotel for a couple of nights. After that, she had arranged to stay at her friend's mother's B&B nearby. I wanted to make it all better for Sarah and Simon but I couldn't.

After a couple of days, I met Sarah for a coffee and suggested that she should come home where I could support her. Eventually, she agreed. So, we went to pack her stuff and I brought her home. She was heartbroken. I felt deeply sorry for her. We spent the next few days drinking gallons of tea, watching 'Friends' and eating chocolate. I didn't press Sarah to find out what happened between them. Even though Simon was heartbroken, he refused to take Sarah back. It was such a sad situation.

After a few weeks, Sarah left her job at the hotel. She found a new job in Wells for the time being. It was too awkward working at the hotel, especially with Simon working close by in the gym. He still had their little dog Brutus, though it was becoming more difficult for Simon to look after him; as he was doing longer shifts this meant that he had to leave Brutus on his own too often. Simon told me that he was going to have to find a new home for Brutus. I couldn't bear that. I knew how much they both loved Brutus, so I offered to take him for a while. I thought it may help Sarah if she had Brutus with us. I was aware that Paul wouldn't be happy about it, but I couldn't let Simon rehome this dog. So, Brutus came to live with us. The cat wasn't too chuffed, yet after a few spats, they got used to each other.

Owen and I became really fond of Brutus. We would often walk him together after my workday finished. Owen used to confide in me while we were out walking. He told me that he was becoming scared of Paul and was worried about his strange behaviour. I reassured him that I would never let his dad do anything to hurt him and that everything would be okay. I said that I was going to sort something out. I had a plan. That was when I realized that it was time to start seriously considering leaving Paul.

One evening, when we were walking Brutus, Owen kept looking behind us. When I turned around, I saw Paul following us. Every time we stopped or looked around, Paul disappeared behind a tree or a parked car. It was completely bizarre. Owen was alarmed and I promised him that I would make sure that we got out of this situation. I explained that I had decided what I was going to do. I made it clear to Owen that we all needed to keep Paul as calm as we could, just for the next few weeks. This would give me time to find us somewhere else to live. Owen said that he would do all he could to help me. That same night, I told Sarah that I was making plans to leave Paul. She was beyond relieved and said that she would help me too.

So, the next day, I began to look at houses to rent. I found a lovely one. It was on the other side of Minehead, far away from Paul. I was confident that I could afford it so I decided to take it. The downside was, that we couldn't move in for six weeks. We would have to keep as quiet as we could about it. I couldn't risk Paul discovering my escape plan. God knows what he would do. Each day, we kept him as calm as we could although the atmosphere at home was very tense. I was so anxious all the time. Most nights we would stay in the bedroom watching television while Paul was sifting through paperwork or fiddling around with insurance policies. He appeared to be obsessed with getting his affairs in order.

About four weeks after I had signed up for the new house, it was a beautiful evening so I decided to take Brutus for a quick walk before

I made dinner. Sarah was at work, as was Paul. Owen said that he would come with me. We enjoyed our walks and talking time. It was good for Owen to be able to talk openly, without his dad within earshot. Brutus was a lively little dog, and he seemed unsettled that day. He was barking most of the way and pulling on the lead, more than usual. He seemed really agitated and began to dart around all over the path. I found him difficult to control.

We decided to go a bit further than we had planned, along towards the church. There was some grass there, so we could let Brutus off the lead. As we walked, his barking became incessant and he kept on lunging towards the road. He was a strong little fella. I was struggling to control him. He was barking furiously at a massive lorry which was coming towards us. I shouted his name in an attempt to calm him down. Then I gave the lead a quick pull hoping to stop him. At this point, Owen was walking behind me. The lead was cutting into my hand so I tried to swap hands. Just as I did, the lead slipped out of my hands. I panicked. It was slipping away from me. I started to run to grab hold of it, but I couldn't reach it. Brutus was racing too far in front of us, barking frantically at the lorry swiftly coming towards us.

Suddenly, everything seemed to be moving in slow motion. Brutus was heading straight towards the front of the lorry. I desperately shouted, 'Brutus' 'Brutus' over and over again, as loud as I could. I couldn't get him to stop. He was on a mission. He kept running towards the lorry, barking, and barking, By this point, I was screaming at him to stop. I shouted and waved my arms in the air, hoping to get the lorry driver's attention, too. It was too late, the driver couldn't stop in time. I froze on the spot, completely. I couldn't take it in.

The lorry driver tried to stop but he didn't see Brutus until it was too late. This was a nightmare, I would wake up in a minute. I stared at Brutus' body. Finally, the lorry came to a grinding halt. I saw it all, everything. I screamed and burst into tears. When I looked behind me, Owen was on the ground. He was lying on his stomach, screaming, and crying. He was bashing both his wrists on the ground and flapping his legs. He was repeating, "No, no, no! This isn't happening."

I couldn't cope. I lost control and kept on screaming. I couldn't stop. I rushed over to Owen and picked him up. I hugged him and turned his face away from the lorry. I hoped to God that he hadn't seen the same as I had. I looked up into the cab of the lorry. The driver was in shock with his head cupped in his hands. He was crying, too. Within minutes, a woman came out of a house opposite the accident. She had heard the commotion. I was beside myself. I blamed myself, it was all my fault. This was a living hell. How would we all get over such a trauma?

How on earth was I going to tell Sarah and Simon? Owen was inconsolable. He couldn't stop crying. He slumped back down on the ground. I didn't know which way to turn. I wanted desperately to turn back the clock. We were both shaking. I walked over to the wall and held on to it. I felt like I was going to pass out. I looked up to the sky and shouted, "This can't be happening!"

I tried to pick Owen up again but he kept slipping through my arms. My heart was pounding, I knew I had to try and pull myself together for Owen's sake. It was all so horrific. The woman from the house came over to us both. I noticed that she was crying, too. She guided us into her house and we sat down in the kitchen. She made us some tea but I couldn't focus on anything. I kept mumbling, "No, no! This can't be happening."

I couldn't process such a nightmare. Owen stopped crying and was sitting on the kitchen chair, staring at the floor. I knew he was traumatised. The woman was talking to him, but he didn't reply. I heard her say that she had recognised him from school. She said that she was the Head of English. She asked Owen his name. He didn't respond at all. He was in a trance. I kept wondering how he would ever get over this. A few minutes later, it dawned on me that I would have to tell Sarah and Simon. I just didn't know how. The woman asked me if there was anyone she could call. Eventually, I found the words to tell her that I needed to call my daughter and her ex-boyfriend. I explained that Brutus was their dog. I burst into tears again at the thought of telling them. It was all too much. They were going to be devastated. I was convinced that they would blame me. I was worried that Sarah would never forgive me.

I couldn't wait any longer. I mustered up the courage from somewhere and called Simon. When he picked up the phone and I heard his chirpy voice, I couldn't speak. I managed to squeak out my name. He kept asking me what was wrong. I could only mumble 'Brutus.' He asked me where I was. I told him there had been a terrible accident. He choked up. I told him I was so, so, sorry, I whispered that I couldn't stop him, and that he had run out in front of a lorry. The phone went silent but I could hear Simon crying. He took a huge breath and came back on the line. I told him we were in a house along the road near the church. He told me that he was coming straightaway. I think he thought that Brutus was injured, but still alive. Before I could explain, or even find the words to tell him that he was dead, Simon had ended the call, and was on his way.

One of the police officers came to the house. He had tears in his eyes and told us that he would arrange for someone to take Brutus away. He said that he was deeply sorry. He had not seen anything like it before. I struggled to believe that, but by the look on his face, I did. He looked ashen and shocked. He said that he had a dog and if anything like that had happened to his dog, he would be in the same state as we were now. He turned and left.

Simon arrived within minutes. I heard him shouting. When I went out to see what was happening, Simon was being pulled away from the lorry and Brutus's covered body on the ground. Simon was desperately trying to get to Brutus. He was explaining that he owned the dog. He said that he needed to take him to the vet. The policeman was trying to tell him that it was too late, but Simon wouldn't listen. They wouldn't let him go any further. Simon was crying and threw his hands in the air. He walked around in circles, then he came over to me. That's when he realised. I burst into tears again and kept saying that I was so sorry. He gave me a hug and we both sobbed. Owen was still silent. Just sitting there still staring at the floor. Simon gave him a reassuring pat on the back as he walked past him and sat down at the table with Owen. I gathered myself together enough to tell him what had happened.

Simon was so understanding. He told me that I must not blame myself. He said that Brutus was nuts and that he had a death wish. He said that it could have happened anytime to any one of us. I felt a tiny bit better hearing that, until I remembered that we still had to tell Sarah. I couldn't face her. I cried every time I imagined her face. Simon asked where Sarah was. I told him that she was at work. Without hesitation, he told me not to worry and said that he would tell her. I was so grateful to him for that.

Later Simon shared with me that before he had the chance to speak, Sarah asked him what had happened to Brutus; even though she knew instinctively. Simon broke down and told her that he had been in a terrible accident while he was out with Owen and me. Simon told her that he had run in front of a lorry. As I expected, Sarah was completely devasted. Thank God she didn't ask any more questions. She seemed to accept that Brutus had gone bonkers, like Simon mentioned to me.

Eventually, Owen and I walked home. I was clutching Brutus's lead. It was strange not to have this beautiful dog with us as we approached home. The thought of calling Paul hadn't crossed my mind. He was quite simply the last person on my mind. When we went into the house, we went straight into the lounge and sat together in silence. There were just no words. After a while I rang Paul. I started crying again when I tried to tell him what had happened.

Paul didn't like it when I cried. Angrily, he snapped, "Pull yourself together! Nothing can be that bad." I managed to tell him what had happened between sobs. My heart was breaking. Callously, he snapped, "Well, we have loads of dog food left. Maybe we can use it for a shepherd's pie." Unbelievable! Paul didn't understand that we were traumatised. Owen and I had watched our pet, Brutus die a horrible death. He had been ripped apart just like our hearts were being now. I reasoned that Paul must have been so traumatised by being part of the Troubles in Ireland and its aftermath that he was hardened to death. Painfully he showed no compassion towards his son nor me. He didn't even ask if Owen was alright. I was speechless. I ended the call, quickly.

Sarah and Simon arrived shortly after that phone conversation. As soon as I saw them, I burst into tears as they came through the door. We all just stood in the hallway crying and hugging each other. After a while, tearfully, Sarah said, "I know what he's like, Mum. You shouldn't blame yourself." Thank God at least for Sarah's generous spirit. We all sat together in the lounge and after crying some more we all sat in silence with our own thoughts.

CHAPTER 4

Suspicion Rising 2010

Sarah and I were at home when we heard on the radio that a local man had been arrested in possession of a shotgun. Without speaking, Sarah and I rushed out of the kitchen and into the hallway to check that Paul's shotgun was still there. It was, thank God. We were convinced that the man in the news, was Paul. That was the moment when I realized, that if we were this alarmed about Paul we had to get out of that house. Unfortunately, there were still three weeks until we could move into our new home. We discussed our plans when Paul wasn't there. I began to wonder whether he was recording us. I wouldn't have put that past him. He used to record conversations at work on his phone. Paul was truly slipping into his own world of paranoia. Because he could have been recording us, to be on the safe side, we began texting each other, instead of talking. This situation was becoming urgent. We were constantly on edge. I urged Sarah and Owen to stay positive. I reassured them both that we would all soon be away from this situation.

Paul was constantly trying to provoke arguments. It became mentally exhausting. He would start an argument about a programme being shown on the TV. He questioned and twisted everything we talked about. It was emotionally draining. I just couldn't stand it a second longer. I had a feeling that he had guessed that we were planning our escape. He seemed to be trying to provoke a response from me, so that I would admit our plan. Paul started talking about people at work, saying that they were planning to leave their partners. It seemed like he was trying to get me to slip up and tell him something.

Often, the three of us would drive to the beach and sit in the car to talk. At least there, we had no risk of him hearing or recording us. I shared with Sarah and Owen the arrangements and timing for moving into the rented house. A couple of friends were at the ready to help us move. Of course, we had to do it while Paul was at work. Hoping and praying that he wouldn't get find out and turn up in the middle of our escape. Sarah and Owen couldn't wait to be out of that house.

Paul had just bought a rowing boat. It was a Sunday morning, when he suggested that Owen go out in the boat. Just the two of them. Owen and I panicked. Owen immediately said that he didn't want to go. Paul flew into a rage. He bolted across the room and pushed Owen backwards into a chair. He got right up into Owen's face and snarled at him, saying that he was a mummy's boy. I could see that Owen was terrified. He burst into tears and pleaded for Paul to get off him. I was furious. I pulled Paul away from Owen and stood in between them. I shouted at Paul to leave Owen alone. I told him that there was no way Owen was going on that boat! Paul was livid, and wild. He had that terrifying look in his eyes. He stomped out of the house, shouting that he was going to drive into the nearest lake. Sarah was in her bedroom. When she heard the door slam, she ran into the lounge and burst into tears. She said that she had an awful feeling that Paul was going to come back and hurt us all. I actually had the same feeling, even though I didn't want to admit it. We had nowhere to go for at least two more weeks. What could I do?

After a few hours, Paul was still out. I started to worry that he had driven into the lake. I called the police to report what had happened earlier and that Paul had disappeared. I told the police that he had threatened to drive into a lake. When I told them about Paul terrifying Owen and getting up into his face, they were concerned. They told me that Paul could be charged for an assault on a minor. I told them about his recent behaviour and that I was seriously concerned about his mental health. They agreed to check out the lake and promised me that they would call me as soon as they knew anything. The police called back within the hour to confirm that they had found Paul standing at the edge of the lake. They said that they talked to him for a while and managed to convince him to seek help from the doctor. They warned me that he would be coming home soon. I was terrified. I had involved the police.

About half an hour later, Sarah, Owen, and I were in the lounge watching TV when suddenly Paul appeared in the hallway. He must have driven to the house without his lights on. We were startled to see him standing there. I wanted to take him away from Sarah and Owen so I went into the kitchen, and he followed me. Strangely calm, he mentioned that he had spoken to the police and that he had agreed to go to the doctors the next day. I was pleased that he was going to get some help. He seemed subdued and he didn't want to talk. He laid down on one of the sofas in the lounge, muttering random words to himself.

Sarah and Owen were both sitting at the dining table in the lounge. Sarah was wearing a hoodie with the hood up over her head. We were all texting each other frantically. Suddenly, Paul jumped up off the sofa and stomped into the garden. We heard banging and clattering outside. He was throwing things out of the shed and all over the lawn. He started to hammer a great big post into the ground muttering to himself. Sarah was silently crying at the table. She and Owen were texting me, saying that we needed to get out of there. They were both scared that he was going to kill us all. I was frightened too. I assured them that we would be okay and told them to keep quiet. When Paul marched back into the house, he was manic. He had that wild look in his eyes, again. He darted into the lounge and started ripping through all the drawers in the dressers. He was raking through papers, saying that he was looking for his Will and his insurance policies. He couldn't find them. I tried to calm him down and asked him why he needed them. He kept mumbling, making no sense, then he pushed passed me.

I knew that we were in trouble. Sarah and Owen were rigid with fear. They couldn't move from the table. I texted them both that I was going into the bedroom to call the police. Paul was frantically darting everywhere. He was in and out of the house, garage, the shed, and throwing things all over the place. I was terrified that he was going to get hold of the gun. I didn't know if it was loaded. While he was outside, I managed to grab the gun and slide it under Sarah's bed. I rang the police. I couldn't speak very loudly but I managed to whisper that my husband had gone off the rails. I told them that I was frightened that he was going to harm my two children and me. They told me to stay calm and bring the kids with me into one room. They said that I should hold tight until they arrived. They assured me that they were sending a patrol car, straightaway. They said that they would turn off the headlights when they arrived at the house. They would then quietly tap on the door. They told me to let them in silently when they arrived.

While Paul was in the garden, I did as the police said and shut the door. We huddled on the bed. Sarah was in floods of tears. She kept saying that he was going to kill us. Owen kept silent. It seemed like hours before I heard the police tap on the front door. I left Sarah and Owen in the bedroom and quietly crept into the hallway. Suddenly, Paul appeared in front of me. He stared at me as if he knew what was happening. He rushed passed me to the bedroom, ignoring Sarah and Owen, thank God. He ripped open the base of the wardrobe and took the Rolex watch and his dad's dress ring and shoved them into his pocket. Next, he went into the lounge and grabbed his Will and insurance policies.

By this time, I had opened the door and the police were inside. Paul stood in the lounge doorway with his hands out in front of him and he almost looked relieved. One of the two police officers asked if I was okay. I answered, "Yes." The other asked where Sarah and Owen were. I told him that they were in the bedroom and that they were also okay. One of the policemen brought Paul and me into the lounge. The other policeman went to check on Sarah and Owen. Paul was quiet. The policeman asked Paul about his erratic and threatening behaviour towards my family. He denied it. He started getting agitated. He gave me a filthy look. The policeman told him to calm down while he continued questioning him. At which point he asked me to go and check on Sarah and Owen, which I did. I sat down on the bed with Sarah and Owen and the other policeman. I hardly dared to breathe or move. I left the door slightly ajar as I tried to hear what was being said in the lounge.

I could hear Paul telling the policeman that I was lying and that he hadn't done anything wrong. He was arguing with him and he kept telling him to "fuck off." The policeman warned Paul that if he didn't calm down, they would have no choice but to arrest him. Paul barged his way out of the lounge and I heard him heading towards the bedroom. I quickly closed the door and leaned against it. Paul was banging on the door shouting for me to tell the police that there was nothing wrong. I heard the policeman telling him to calm down, again. Paul was shouting for Owen to tell the police that he wasn't scared of him. Owen was petrified. The police managed to move Paul away from the door. They took him back into the lounge and told him to "sit down and shut up!" One of them came back to the bedroom to see us all clearly terrified. I asked him what they could do to help us. He asked Owen if he would be prepared to confirm his dad's actions earlier. If he would, then they would have a valid reason to arrest Paul for assault on a minor. Owen said that he wanted his dad out of the house for all of our sakes, so he agreed.

One policeman handcuffed Paul as the other shielded my kids. What a racket that followed. Paul went ballistic, shouting and screaming that he was going 'to kill us all!' He was calling me a bitch and saying that it was all my fault. The police officers escorted Paul out of the house and into the police car. Sarah, Owen, and I burst into tears of relief as we collapsed on the bed. We were safe, for now.

CHAPTER 5

Two Hours To Leave 2010

What a relief! For the moment Paul had gone from our lives. Naturally, we all felt guilty when he was taken away. I was hoping that Paul would be offered psychiatric help. During my earlier phone call, I had told the police about his strange behaviour over the last few months. I mentioned the stalking, the many recordings of his work colleagues' conversations and his creeping into the house without us knowing. I believed that he would be placed in safe custody for his own safety. He needed professional help. He was, without a doubt, a risk to himself, and us. He had beaten up a stranger in Minehead and he had also gone to the very brink of violence with us at home on too many occasions. I told the police that he was like an unexploded bomb. My kids and I were petrified of him and that I made plans to leave him within the next two weeks. We had been living on a knife edge with him for far too long.

That same night Owen was even more frightened than he was earlier that day. He was scared that if his dad came back soon, he would be angry with him and threaten him again. I hoped that we would have enough time to be able to move out before his dad was released. I had every hope that Paul could be kept away for a couple of weeks. I did my best to comfort Owen after we had talked everything through. We were all emotionally drained. All we wanted to do was to sleep.

All night long I was getting horrendous flashbacks of Brutus's accident. I couldn't shake them off. Every time I closed my eyes the visions came back to me again. Owen was experiencing flashbacks, too. They were awful and vivid. I desperately wanted to sleep, though I daren't close my eyes. I was also afraid that Paul might burst through the doors any minute. The police assured me that they would be able to keep him at least, overnight. Sarah was exhausted with all the stress. She had been sobbing under her hoodie most of the night. Eventually, she fell into bed and went out like a light.

The next morning, I woke up quite early. Owen was already up and watching TV in the lounge. He told me that he was very worried about his dad. He kept saying that he felt guilty as well as scared. I told him that he shouldn't feel guilty and that his dad needed professional help. Hopefully, he would get that now. I said that we had done him a favour. Owen didn't seem convinced, but eventually, he agreed with me.

I rang the police station after a couple of hours around noon to find out what Paul' status was. I was anxious to find out if they had been able to section him. They told me that they had interviewed him for a couple of hours last night. They said that they had continued to interview him this morning. The medical consultant was coming to see him, too. He would be the one to make the final assessment. I told him that we were all terrified about him coming back to the house. I was convinced that he was going to do something terrible. The police officer was very understanding. He assured me that that they would do their best to help us.

I asked how the interview had gone last night. He told me that Paul was aggressive and angry about being arrested. Though, after a while, he calmed down and was quite coherent. They observed that he clearly had issues, though they said that we would need to wait and see what the medical consultant said this afternoon. I was advised to call back in a couple of hours. I had a feeling that they weren't going to be able to keep him away from us. Paul hadn't actually harmed any of us. There was effectively no charge, apart from the assault on a minor which I prayed would be enough to get Paul the help he needed.

To keep myself busy I started clearing up the mess in the garden that Paul had made the night before. I saw that he had thrown things all over the place. The shed looked wrecked with its door hanging off. There were broken jars and snapped pieces of wood scattered everywhere. What a mess! I did my best to get everything back in order. Sarah emerged from her room late morning. It was the first good night's sleep she had had in ages. She was so relieved that Paul had gone. Then, she remembered that he may be coming back. When I told her about my conversation with the police, she really started getting upset, saying, "He can't come back. He will kill us all!" I attempted to calm her down by saying we needed to stay positive. We would find out more when I rang back in a while.

    I had already updated our workplaces about what was happening. Neither Sarah nor I had been back to work since Brutus's accident. I couldn't think straight enough to be able to work. Protecting Sarah and Owen was my priority for now. Philip was as understanding as ever. He had guessed that there was a problem with Paul a while ago. He used to power walk with his wife most evenings. He told me that a couple of times, they became aware of someone behind them. When Philip looked around to see who it was, he was surprised to see Paul. He had been stalking Philip and his wife. Paul would dart behind a tree or a parked car, to stop them from seeing him. Philip hadn't told me at the time as he didn't want to make things worse for me. He knew that Paul was becoming increasingly unhinged. Philip could have reported him for stalking. He thought he was a jealous husband with a bit of a screw loose. Philip hadn't a clue as to the truth. Anyway, he told me that I had enough on my plate and that I should take some time to sort things out. I told him that I had paid the deposit on a rental property, though we couldn't have it for a couple of weeks. He was pleased to hear that we were getting away and asked me to let him know if I needed anything. I was grateful for that.

That afternoon, I rang the police again. To my horror, they informed me that the medical consultant had spoken to Paul for a couple of hours. After which, he didn't consider him a threat. They confirmed that Paul would be released shortly, with a caution. I was horrified! I felt like the earth opened up and dragged me into its muddy darkness. I was shocked that they didn't take him to hospital or anything. I couldn't comprehend the fact that he was coming home in a few hours. I told the police, again how terrified we were. Paul must have been utterly convincing in his act to make them think that he was okay. They said that he had calmed down completely and was lucid. They didn't feel that he posed a threat. How could they have been so fooled? They asked me if the house was jointly owned. I told them that it was his property. They said that they had no choice but to release him and he had every right to come back to his house. They advised me to get out if we didn't feel safe. I told them that we had nowhere to go. I was a hundred percent sure that he would harm us. They kept saying that they were sorry, according to their medical assessment Paul was not a threat. I didn't know what to do.

I was thrown into a complete panic. When I came off the phone, I told Sarah and Owen that we had about two hours to move out. They were both stunned. They asked me what we were going to do. I hadn't a clue. I only had the two-seater car. We could only get a carrier bag of stuff in there!

My mind went blank. The police had advised me to call Social Services to tell them my situation and said that maybe they could arrange temporary accommodation for us. It took me about ten attempts to get through. When I finally reached an actual person, I told them my situation and that we needed urgent help. They told me they would call me back in an hour. In the meantime, we started to pack as many things as we could into bin bags. Sarah was racing around trying to find chargers. Owen packed his play station first! It seemed like the longest hour ever until a different lady from Social Services called back. She told me that they didn't have anything available in Minehead. She offered that they could put us into a hostel in Frome. How was I going to get to Frome with two kids, all our stuff and in a two-seater car? I needed time to think, but I didn't have it. I said I would ring them back and ended the call. Sarah asked what they had said. I told her that they had found us a room at a hostel in Frome. Sarah looked at me, cocked her head to one side, and said, "Hostel, don't you mean Hotel? I don't do hostels. We will end up sitting round in a circle, singing weird songs with women wearing no bras and ginger hair!"

We fell about laughing. That was typical of Sarah. She could always find humour in the worst of times. The way she said things was hilarious. She was mortified at the thought of a hostel! She then remembered her friend Lucy, one of the managers from the hotel in Minehead, where she had worked as a receptionist. She rang Lucy to see if she could organise a room for a night or two. I thought that it was a long shot. We really couldn't afford it but I knew we had to get out before Paul came back. Lucy booked us into a family room. She came straight over in her car to help us pack as many of our clothes and anything else we could fill in both of the cars, within the hour. We raced around the house, desperately trying not to forget the essentials. We rammed everything into bin bags. We loaded up Lucy's car to the brim. We were out of there. Thank God!

As we were leaving one of the neighbours came out. He had seen Paul being taken away the night before. He gave me a massive hug, which was out of character. He never did that.

He was not a huggy type of person. He looked right at me and told me that I was doing the right thing. He wished us luck. My eyes filled with tears. I really didn't want to leave that house. I had grown fond of it and didn't want all this disruption. Who would? I didn't know what was going to happen. All I knew was that we were doing the right thing. We drove away feeling very relieved. We barely made it out of there before Paul got back. I couldn't help wondering how he was going to react when he realized, we had left. Part of me felt guilty for that. He had been good to me at the start. He was ill. He needed help. I couldn't help him anymore. I felt sad that our marriage had broken down, too.

When we checked in to the hotel, the relief was amazing. We were giggling and punch drunk from our newfound freedom. I soon realized though, that we would need to find somewhere else, and soon. I remembered that Philip had told me to ring him if we needed anything at all. So, I rang him and told him that Paul was being released that evening. He wondered how Paul had swung that! I told Philip that we were okay and safe for that night but we needed to find somewhere else to go the next day. Without hesitation, he told me to hang fire and that he would call me back soon. He told me not to worry.

I prayed Philip could help us. Sarah and Owen were messing around downstairs in the hotel bar, acting as if they were on holiday. I went downstairs to join them. It took a while for Philip to call me back. He told me that it was the end of term and the timing couldn't have been better. Most of the students had vacated the university campus. This meant that there would be loads of empty rooms. He had arranged for us to move into J Block the next day. He told me that we could stay for as long as we wanted. He said that apart from some summer lets, there would be nobody else around. He told the security guards at the gates that we were going to be moving in there the next day and he asked them to keep an eye on us. He promised that they would be able to let us know if Paul showed up. I was so grateful. I thanked him a million times. I ended the call and was so relieved that I had a plan. We were sorted. We had somewhere safe for us to stay until we could move into our new home. Sarah and Owen were over the moon when I told them.

    We decided to go for a drive to see the new house. Sarah and Owen hadn't seen where we were moving to yet. I was delighted, as they loved it. They were both happy, at last. I still felt nervous but I was happy about my plan. I drove back to the hotel where we enjoyed some food. We all settled down to watch TV on our comfy hotel beds. That was when I remembered about Paul. I had been so busy working out our plans that I had forgotten about him, and his return to the house. What would he do? Was he home yet? Would he be shocked to find the house empty? I wondered whether he would expect it. All these questions flooded my head. I was becoming extremely anxious about him turning up at the hotel, but I kept quiet. Surely, he wouldn't think that we would be there. I kept thinking that he was so sly, he would somehow work out where we were staying. Thankfully, Sarah and Owen were oblivious to my thoughts and seemed quite relaxed and enjoying their 'hotel holiday.' I decided to keep quiet about my worries and to enjoy our time together.

When we checked out of the hotel the next morning, Lucy followed us to help us move into the campus. Well, when we arrived there, we were delighted. We had the whole of J Block. There were about eight rooms all with ensuite bathrooms, big double beds, wardrobes, and a desk with televisions in every room. There was a kitchen, with a lounge/dining room type space in the communal area. All the rooms were clean. The beds were made up with fresh linens, clean towels were in the bathrooms, and everything we needed was there. It was like a holiday camp. We chose our rooms and started to unpack what little we had. I rang Philip to let him know that we had arrived and that I was beyond grateful to him for his help. He told me to think nothing of it, to keep safe and to stay in touch. He wasn't expecting me back to work until things had calmed down. I told him that I didn't want to let Sarah and Owen out of my sight, now. Philip understood completely, he was a good man. Sarah had told her workplace about the situation. I had spoken to the school to let them know that Owen wouldn't be going in for a while. I told them not to tell Paul anything if he happened to turn up at the school. They agreed.

After we had settled into our rooms, we needed to buy some food. I didn't know what to do about that, as I was worried about being spotted and somebody telling Paul where we were. I rang Paul's work to find out if he had turned up at work and if so, what shift was he on. They told me that he was working on a late shift in Wells. Great news! I plucked up the courage to go to the local supermarket. We all went to the supermarket and each had a trolley. I told Sarah and Owen to get the essentials they needed, as quickly as they could. I said that I would get some food and meet them at the checkout. Well, when we met, we all burst out laughing when we saw what we each had in our trollies. Sarah had an enormous over-sized bowling kit, with a golf set next to it in her trolley. Owen had a cricket kit and a set of footballs in his. I asked them what we were supposed to be doing with those? Sarah said, with a deadpan look on her face, "What else are we going to do with the huge corridor at J Block?" We had fun fitting all our purchases into the boot of the car. We had to stuff things in every gap, including my groceries. Eventually, we managed it. That boot was bigger than it looked! How funny.

When we got back to the campus, we unloaded the shopping and Sarah announced that Simon was coming over to play! I was so pleased to hear that they were still in touch. We spent that night playing corridor bowling, cricket, and golf. It was such a relief to be free of all the tension. I hadn't realized how much pressure we had been living under. The awful circumstances at home with Paul had made us all anxious and scared most of the time. We had forgotten how to have fun. We were making up for that now. It was great to see Sarah, Simon and Owen having a laugh together. Meanwhile, I was experiencing bursts of guilt regarding Paul. I couldn't help being worried about him. I still cared about him, even though he had brought all of this on himself. I kept telling myself that we had no choice and that we had done the right thing. I really hoped that he had seen the doctor to get some help.

Those days at the campus were such fun. It was summer so the weather was great. We managed to get out into the grounds and sit in the sunshine. We played over-sized games in the evenings. We got used to having all the extra space. It was fun hollering at each other from room to room. The security staff got to know us and they were keeping a close eye on us. We felt safe there.

I rang the letting agent to ask if we could take the rental property any sooner. I was elated when they told me that we could have the property a week earlier than planned. Even though we were happy at the campus, I couldn't wait to get into our new home and for the three of us to get on with our lives. I also made an appointment to see a local solicitor. I had made up my mind to divorce Paul as quickly as possible. I wanted out of my second marriage. I thought it would be simple, as the house belonged to Paul. I wouldn't have any claim on it nor would I want one. They said that they would write to Paul to start the ball rolling. Oh no, that thought made me nervous. I was certain that he would flip. I asked them not to give him any indication of where we were staying. I knew that it was only a matter of time before he found us. Paul was like a detective.

Meanwhile back at J Block the laughs kept coming between us all. We had fun with the games, as usual. One night, after I thought we had all gone to bed, I woke up to hear Sarah giggling. Owen and I went into her room to find her sitting on her windowsill with the window open. She told me to look out of her window. There must have been about three hundred Orthodox Jews all riding bikes and walking around. The women were dressed like something out of the TV show, 'Little House on the Prairie.' When we looked up at the building opposite, there was a line of men all bowing their heads. They must have been doing morning prayers. What? Where had they come from? There was no sign of them when we had gone to bed earlier that night. They seemed to be everywhere. Old, young, kids, babies. There were great big black expensive cars and people carriers parked everywhere. It was surreal. Sarah joked, "Have we been beamed into a film set?" Where had they come from? I found out from reception the next day that they had come from two local cities. They came every year for a free fortnight's holiday. They filled up all the campus. I was really surprised that Philip hadn't mentioned it. We found it amusing to see so many people outside of our windows. They didn't engage with us. Perhaps they were on a silent retreat because they didn't seem to chat with each other either. Sarah found them fascinating. She was such fun. Sarah would watch them for hours. It was like being an extra in a film.

As I expected as soon as Paul received the letter from the solicitor, he started ringing me. I didn't want to speak to him. After about fifty of his attempts to contact me, I picked up the call. Immediately, he burst into tears. Oh God, I wasn't prepared for that. Paul asked me, "Can we meet up, please?" I replied, "I don't think that's a good idea, I don't want you to try and talk me into going back to you. Paul, we are getting divorced. There's no way I can stay with you. Not now, not ever." I was determined to go through with the divorce. He was beside himself. "I just want to talk to you... Where are you? Someone said that they had seen you in Asda. So, you are still in Minehead?" he pleaded. I replied, "Minehead? No, no, we 're not there. Paul, promise me that won't try to find us. It's too soon, we are still all terribly upset" "Okay, okay, I promise, though it wouldn't take me long to find you. You know me. I will not try though. But only if you'll meet up with me. I only want to talk to you, like I said." I really didn't want to see him, so I told him that I would think about it. I was nervous about seeing him. I knew I would feel sorry for him, I didn't want to buckle under the pressure. I might, especially if he was crying. He never cried.

We were due to move out of the Campus in a few days. We had finished dinner and Sarah had taken up her usual position at the window in her room watching the activity outside. I heard her shout "Mum, get in here quick." When I got there, she was as white as a sheet. She looked at me and said, "He was out there. He was standing on the grass across the campus looking right in my window straight at me. Mum... I'm scared..." Oh my God, Paul had found us. I rushed outside to see if I could see him, he had vanished.

CHAPTER 6

It's Over 2010

Paul, crafty as ever, managed to convince the security men on the gate that we had arranged for him to visit Owen. I rang my solicitor straightaway to tell her that he had turned up. What might he do next? She told me that she would send a warning letter out to Paul immediately telling him to stay away from us. If he didn't, we would then draw up a restraining order. I hoped that the warning would be enough to stop him, though I doubted he would even read the letter. Paul thought he was above the law.

We were all nervous after that. We were convinced that he was watching our every move. I was extremely relieved when we finally got the keys to our new house. I felt quite proud of myself that I had managed to get us safely through all this carnage. A couple of friends offered to help us move. We loaded up the cars and handed the keys to J Block into the gatehouse. Even though we were enjoying our time at J Block, and we were so grateful to Philip. We were looking forward to having our own home.

It was ideal; a new townhouse with three floors. I had the top floor with its large attic bedroom and ensuite bathroom. All the cream coloured carpets were new and the walls were freshly painted. I loved it. At last, somewhere of my own. I couldn't wait to make it our cosy home. It was an open plan design downstairs and there was a small garden with a patio, at the back of the house. I had a great feeling about it from the minute I originally saw it. Sarah and Owen loved it, too. They both had big bedrooms. The house was partly furnished. I had managed to save a few pounds each month to fund our house move. It wouldn't last long, though it was enough to get us started with bedding and other bits and bobs.

My solicitor told me that even though I wasn't named on the marital house deeds, I was entitled to get something from the marriage with Paul. It was not my usual style, yet I needed to be able to make a home for Sarah and Owen. So, I told her I agreed. She was determined to achieve a fair settlement for me. She said that she would send another letter to Paul, telling him my intention to divorce him was on the grounds of his unreasonable behaviour. I instructed her to make it perfectly clear to Paul that I didn't want him to sell the house. It was important that the house should go to Owen, eventually.

As I expected, when the letter landed on Paul's doorstep, the very first thing he did was to ask me to meet him. I hadn't seen him for ages so I didn't feel that I could avoid him any longer. I agreed to meet him in a restaurant in Wells. I certainly didn't want to be alone with him. Most probably he would keep his cool if there were other people around. When I arrived at the restaurant, Paul was waiting for me. He was dressed in a badly fitted suit, with a silk shirt and tie, holding a single red rose. Oh dear!

   I chuckled to myself. He looked ridiculous. The suit jacket was oversized and the trousers were too tight. I think he had walked into a charity shop with sunglasses on and picked the nearest thing to a suit he could find. Paul was never any good at colour coordination. Once I composed myself, I went over to him. He tried to give me a hug. I backed away from him and sat down. He flung the rose at me and then started rambling on. He went off on a right tangent. In amongst his wall of words, he told me that he understood why I had him arrested that night. He said that he forgave me for that. Wait, What? Paul was talking nonstop for ages trying to justify his paranoid behaviour over the last few months. Mostly, he tried to blame Sarah or me for the way he had been acting. I was not buying any of it. Eventually, after he had talked for what felt like hours, I managed to get a word in. I asked him if he had been getting any professional help, or counselling. He told me that he had seen a counsellor a couple of times, though the counsellor was rubbish. He decided he wasn't going to go back again.

I think what Paul really meant was, that the counsellor was telling him a few home truths and he couldn't take it. He wasn't great at taking advice from anybody. He kept saying that he still loved me, and that he wanted me back. He said that he would change. He promised that he wouldn't do anything to hurt any of us. Eventually, he asked about Owen. I told him that Owen was fine, but he was scared of him. Astonishingly, Paul couldn't understand why. He didn't understand that his behaviour had not only been bizarre, but it had also been terrifying for us all. Paul seemed to think that it was normal behaviour. In his world maybe, but not ours.

Paul kept asking me to tell him where we were living. He knew that we had moved from the campus. He confirmed that he had received the letter from my solicitor instructing him to keep away from us. He said that he was upset about that, though he agreed that he would keep away. He said that he had every right to know where we were living. Especially, as regards to his son, Owen. He kept trying to hold my hand across the table so I firmly placed them on my knees. He asked me how I was going to manage on my own, financially. I told him not to worry about that as I had it all covered. I told him that Sarah would be helping me with the rent. He didn't seem to like that very much. He didn't take the opportunity to ask how Sarah was, either.

It became perfectly clear to me at this point, that Paul was worried that I wanted him to sell the house. He should have known me better. Without prompting, he brought up that he had no intention to sell the house. He said that I wasn't entitled to make him do that, as it was his house. I didn't need him to tell me that. Paul seemed to be focusing on just talking about money. I told him that my solicitor would be dealing with the finances and that I was leaving all of that to her. My solicitor said that legally, I was entitled to something, as I was looking after Owen and we had been married over ten years. He smiled, shrugged his shoulders, and said, "That may change." As if he knew something I didn't. He said that he would be instructing a solicitor the next day. He declared that he would fight me tooth and nail against selling the house. He wasn't listening, as usual. I told him that there was nothing to fight about because I didn't want him to sell the house. I repeated that I wanted the house to be left for Owen. He talked over me constantly. I could tell he wasn't hearing me, he was concentrating on what he was going to say. He started getting agitated.

I warned him that if he didn't calm down, I would leave. His eyes filled with tears. He told me he didn't want to agree to a divorce. He didn't want to rush into a divorce. He asked me to wait to save the solicitors' costs for both of us. He was all over the place. One minute he was angry and stubborn, the next minute he was in tears and begging me to go back to him. He told me that he didn't think when we got married, it would end in divorce. He said that he had married me for life and I should have done the same. I explained that sometimes things don't work out. I didn't trust him anymore. I said that I couldn't live with someone so volatile. I didn't want to live in fear of him doing something dangerous. He promised me again that he would change.

When it was becoming clear to him that he was getting nowhere with me, he changed his tactic. He started to tell me that most of it was my fault. He said that I had been distant with him. He thought that I should have thanked him for putting up with my kids, and all their problems over the years. He said that he had been good to us, and that we should be grateful to him. I agreed with him that he had been good to us in the early years. I was grateful for that, but he had changed. He now was becoming relentless. Between bites, he kept insisting that we get back together. After a while, I couldn't stand it. I got sick of hearing the same words. Eventually, I blurted out that it was never going to happen. I told him that I didn't love him anymore.

We were getting nowhere so I got up and left him at the restaurant. As I left, I heard him say that he would find me. I was nervous all the way home as I was convinced that he would follow me. I felt that he already knew where we lived and that he was trying to get me to confirm it. I was suspicious.

I rang my solicitor first thing the next day and instructed her to go ahead with the divorce. It wasn't long before Paul started to sell things for cash so there would be no trace. Not only did he sell the Rolex watch and the dress ring, but he also sold the classic car as well. He said that he had got a cash buyer for it. Owen was gutted as he loved that car and it had been left to him by his Grandad. Paul didn't care about that. I was furious and made him promise me that he would put the value of the car, about £10,000 into an account for Owen. At least he would have that instead of the car. Of course, that meant that Paul had much less wealth than I had listed to the solicitor. I didn't really care about that. I thought it was typical of Paul to start selling things, to block me from getting any of it. I was surprised that he thought it was about the money for me. It made me sad that he didn't know me better than that.

We still needed to get a few things for our house. Sarah and I decided to go out shopping one day while Owen was at school. The first thing Sarah insisted we bought was a gold dinner set. She plonked it straight into the trolley, saying it was imperative that we have it. We filled the trolley, including a great big, framed mirror for the lounge. Then we realized we only had a two-seater car. We stuffed as much as we could into the boot, in the foot well and under the soft top behind us. Just one item was left over, the great big mirror. Sarah had the bright idea to sit in the passenger seat while I passed her the mirror. She could then rest it on her knees. We tried all different ways to get it into the car. Finally, Sarah managed to squeeze it lengthways between her legs and wedged it underneath her neck. It was hilarious. We couldn't do much apart from laugh. Before we set off, Sarah turned her head and said, with a straight face, "For God's sake don't brake hard, or you will slit my throat with this thing." We laughed all the way home and I never braked once. When we got home, I managed to peel her out of the car. After that, we unloaded all of our treasures. It was so good to be so relaxed. We were free from all the tension we had been through with Paul. Everything seemed a breeze and funny to us at that time. It was so liberating.

    A day or two later, the flat pack furniture arrived. I set about assembling the glass dining table. Sarah built a wardrobe for her bedroom. It had a wooden frame with a canvas cover. We thought this would be simple enough. Sarah was over the moon when she finished. She announced that she had done it. When she put it in position, she discovered that she had built it upside down. Hilarity set in again! She quickly rebuilt it. Owen decided he would help by assembling a small glass coffee table. For some reason though, he built it around himself and ended up stuck inside the frame. Those were such fun times. We were all getting along like a house on fire. Loving our freedom.

Next, we needed a three-piece suite, so I ordered a tasteful, deep brown suede one. It looked ideal in the brochure. Sarah went out early on the day it was due to arrive. The suite was delivered as arranged. I couldn't believe it. It was miniature. It didn't fill the lounge at all. I couldn't help but laugh when I started to unpack it. I kept moving it around the lounge to try to make it look bigger. Owen looked huge when he sat on it. We were both in hysterics. When Sarah came home later that afternoon, she strolled in, took one look at the furniture, and said, "I'm sorry, have I come to the wrong house? Is this the Sylvania family cottage?" All of us fell about laughing. Simon lived nearby so Sarah rang him straightaway. She asked him to come quick as she needed help with something. He looked so funny sitting on the sofa. Like Will Ferrell when he played Elf in the film! We all fell about laughing, trying different ways to make it look bigger. I finally realized that I had just made a mistake. Even though the comedy value was fantastic, I arranged for it to go back. I replaced it quickly with a more suitable sofa.

Sarah changed her job and started working

at the university. She called herself a 'dinner lady' but she was much more than that. She loved the job, and the people. Sarah made friends there immediately. She quickly became extremely popular and worked hard. She went out socially with her friends regularly, too.

Owen was spending much of his time with his best friend, Tim. They got on well and played games on his play station. I was surprised when I found out that Owen had also been seeing his dad without telling me. Paul took great delight in informing me that he had been ringing Owen when I wasn't around. Owen had already asked me if he could spend the occasional weekend with Paul. I was concerned because Owen had told me that he was scared of Paul. When I spoke to Owen about it, he admitted that he missed his dad. He said that he didn't feel as scared of him as he had before. He told me that he wanted to start seeing a bit more of him. I was worried about it, but Owen insisted that his dad was calmer and he wanted to see him. I decided to agree to the visits but stressed to Owen that if he ever felt unsafe and wanted to come home, I would collect him, immediately.

Owen assured me that he was fine so he started staying with Paul on the alternate weekends. They seemed to be enjoying car shows. Owen really enjoyed it. After a while, Owen became much happier and I was confident that he was safe spending time with

Paul. Sarah was taking up plenty of my time. I had fun being 'mum's taxi' after she had been to the cinema or out with her friends. I tried to split my time equally between Owen and Sarah. I missed my dog walks with Owen. We used to talk so much when we had that time together. We did have fun watching films and eating chocolate buttons.

It was Monday morning, and I was taking Owen to school, then going to work. When he got in the car, he announced that he had left his PE kit at Paul's. He said that he had taken it there after school on Friday. He remembered that he didn't have it with him when he came back to me on Sunday. Owen seemed edgy and told me that he must pick it up before he went to school. Otherwise, he would be in trouble. I agreed to pick it up and drop him at school afterwards. On the way, Owen assured me that Paul wasn't there and that he had his key to get in the house. Owen promised me that there was no chance that I would see Paul. When we arrived at Paul's house, I had hardly stopped the car before Owen bolted straight into the house and closed the front door. As he disappeared, I was telling him to be quick and that I would wait in the car. Owen was in there for what felt like ages.

As time was racing on, I decided to knock on the door. Paul answered. I was shocked when I saw him. I asked him what Owen was doing.

I explained that we were late for school. Paul calmly looked right at me and announced that Owen wasn't coming. What?? I shouted for Owen and he appeared behind Paul. I was so confused. I asked them both what was going on. Paul urged me to go away. He repeated that Owen wasn't coming. I panicked and said that I needed to take him to school. Paul kept telling me to go away. I tried to talk to Owen, but he had disappeared into the kitchen. I shouted for Owen to come with me. I tried to get past Paul to get to Owen but he stopped me. He said that if I tried to go any further, he would call the police. I was panic stricken and desperate to get to Owen. Owen started shouting that I should leave. What? I couldn't understand what was happening. Finally, Paul explained that Owen had told him that he had been unhappy for ages living with Sarah and me. Paul and Owen had planned this. Owen hadn't left his PE kit. This was like a knife through my heart, I couldn't process it. After all, Owen had begged me to leave Paul over all those months. How could this be happening? I simply wasn't prepared to lose Owen. Paul had always promised me that he would never do this to me. After a few minutes, Paul slammed the door in my face. I banged on the door shouting for Owen to come out. Paul just repeated that I should go away, or he would call the police. I was getting nowhere so I decided I must leave Owen with Paul. For now, anyway. I fell into my car and broke down. How was I going to cope without Owen? I wasn't.

CHAPTER 7

Losing Owen

How I drove back home without crashing the car, I just don't know. I was hysterical. When I got home, I burst through the door and ran straight upstairs into Sarah's room. She was asleep under a pile of clothes. She immediately woke up when I collapsed on the bed crying. I couldn't pull myself together. She sprung into action and asked me what on earth was wrong. I explained to her that Owen was gone. I cried out that Owen had gone back to Paul and that they must have planned it. Sarah was shocked. She hadn't seen this coming, either. Neither of us could figure out what had happened or work out what to do. I explained that I had done everything I could to persuade Owen to come back with me. It was impossible because I couldn't get past Paul. He was blocking the doorway. They both kept telling me to go away, and that if I didn't, Paul would call the police. I believed that he would and I had to drive away whether I liked it or not.

Sarah suggested that she should call Tyler and ask him to speak to Owen. Sarah thought that Tyler may be able to persuade him to come back, or at the very least let us know what's really going on. I couldn't believe that Owen would do this, especially after everything we had been through. Now, the guilt set in. I questioned whether I had been concentrating too much on Sarah. Maybe I hadn't spent enough time with Owen. It must have been my fault, somehow. I felt like such a bad mother. Could I have been that clueless?

I constantly rang Owen but he didn't answer my calls. Sarah spoke to Tyler and explained what had happened. Tyler was shocked and said that he would call Owen. Though, it didn't feel right involving Tyler. I was desperate and I would do anything to get Owen back. Or at least find out what the problem was. I had never been separated from Owen since the day he was born. I felt terrible when I realized that Owen must have been unhappy living with us.

I made an appointment that day with my solicitor to inform her that Owen had gone back to Paul. She said that in her opinion, Owen was old enough as he was thirteen to make his own decisions about where he wanted to be. She explained that there was little I could do about it. She suggested that I remain hopeful about Owen's return to Sarah and me.

The next few days trying to get hold of Owen were hell. Then finally, Paul rang me. He informed me that because Owen was back with him, he wanted the Government child benefit redirected to his bank account. Oh my god things just went from bad to worse. I refused to agree to that, as I wanted Owen back with me. I reminded him that he had promised me he would never do this. Paul blamed me, saying that I had 'blown it' with Owen. He said that Owen wasn't happy living with us. He wanted to be back in his old room. Owen had made it clear to Paul that he didn't like our new house. I found it difficult to believe Paul. I asked to speak to Owen myself but Paul refused, saying that Owen didn't want to speak to me. I was beyond desperate to speak to Owen. I missed him terribly. I was also worried that Paul was influencing Owen against me; not to mention that I was worried about Owen's safety.

I began to wonder if this had been one of Paul's schemes for the last few weeks to cause trouble between Sarah and me. I even considered that Paul was manipulating me to go back to him, especially now that Owen was there. I was so torn. For a brief moment I did consider going back to Paul. Fortunately, I quickly came back to my senses, and realized that of course it would be madness!

Before Owen left, I decided to arrange a big party for my fiftieth birthday. Once we had our newfound freedom from Paul, I felt that we finally had something to celebrate. I booked a gorgeous harbourside bar. I hoped that the party would be an ideal opportunity to bring us all back together. Now that Owen was with Paul, this was all the more important. Little Eileen and

Carol agreed to join us. I had splashed out and bought a dress for Sarah, a suit for Owen and a lovely dress for me.

Tyler and Minnie were coming to stay for a week before the party. I began to really look forward to it. This would be a chance to have all my three kids together. This opportunity was not to be missed. I invited all the family but unfortunately, they couldn't make it, mainly because of the distance. The journey was far too much for Mam, especially. I had quite a few friends at the university and they would be coming. When Owen discovered that Tyler was coming down for a week before the party, he was delighted and immediately agreed to come home for that week, too. I was thrilled! I was secretly hoping that I could persuade Owen to stay with me after the party.

We all had a wonderful week together. We went for long walks, spent time on the beach, played games and had lovely long lunches by the ocean, too. It was so good spending such precious time together. We made some memories to treasure. Tyler looked incredibly well, and joyful. He and Minnie were such a sweet couple. It was heart-warming to see Tyler's health so much improved. I was delighted to observe that he had tons of energy, and a huge appetite, too. The band were doing exceptionally well, with loads of performances booked. What brilliant news to hear! After all that Tyler had been through, nobody deserved success more than he did.

On the day of the party, everyone congregated at my house. It felt like a wedding. Paul knew about the party, but I asked him not to show up. He agreed not to come anywhere near the party. I didn't want him to ruin my special day. About an hour before the party, we were all having our pictures taken, when there was a knock on the door. When I answered it, there stood a neighbour I had not yet met. She was holding a huge bouquet of flowers, with a smile on her face. She slowly turned and pointed up the road. There was Paul. He was standing there looking awkward and waving at me. The lovely lady explained that Paul had knocked on her door and asked her to pass on the flowers to me.

I felt sorry for him. He looked pathetic standing there on his own. So, I waved back. After all, the flowers were a thoughtful thing to do. I couldn't help thinking however, that there was an ulterior motive with Paul. Things were never as they appeared to be where he was concerned. Thank God, Paul kept away from the party, as promised. Though, I heard later that he had been sitting in the pub across the road, watching us. Typical!

We had arranged for a professional photographer to attend the party. She began by taking lots of photographs of us at the house before we set off to the venue. Once we arrived, she took random photos of all the guests as they enjoyed the evening. We had a wonderful time. It was fantastic to have all my kids together, too. They each read small tributes, saying lovely things about me. I was extremely happy and immensely proud of them. It was amazing to have most of my good friends together, too. Especially those from the North who had made a special effort to be with me. What a brilliant night.

Once Tyler and Minnie had left to return home, Owen dropped the bombshell that he wanted to go back to Paul's house. I tried my utmost to persuade him to stay but he explained that he felt sorry for Paul. He assured me that Paul would take care of him and that he would be alright. He wasn't afraid of him anymore because Paul had calmed down and they were becoming car buddies. He was genuinely worried about Paul being alone. I was proud of my Owen and thought that this was very mature of him but I was also so amazed that all of this could change so fast. It felt like this all came from nowhere. Even though, I was sad that he felt this burden I decided that at this time I would let him go. At thirteen, he was old enough to make his own decisions. Though, I missed him very much and I hated the whole situation. Owen had been spending more time with Paul than with Sarah and me. He explained that he preferred to go to car shows, or mess around in the garage with Paul than visit us. That hurt, but I respected that Owen shared his love of cars with his dad. It made sense that he would prefer to be there. I understood all of that. I chose to accept this for Owen's sake, for now.

PART TWO

THE AMERICAN DREAM

CHAPTER 8

Curiosity & Temptation 2011

Even though I missed him, Owen seemed to be getting along fine with Paul. He was settling back into a school routine, too. We were seeing him as much as we could. Sarah was loving life and enjoying her job at the university. Tyler had embarked on a tour with the band and they were flying high.

Everything finally seemed to be calming down for us all. I discovered the joys of Facebook and began to spend more time on there in the evenings. I enjoyed reconnecting with old friends, and making new ones, too. As with most people, occasionally, I received rather odd messages, mostly from men. I ignored or deleted most of them. This particular one was a beauty. How crazy is this? 'Are you ready to be a superstar?' popped into my Messenger App. I couldn't help but laugh out loud. At first, I ignored it. But then intrigue kicked in and I had a look at the profile. It was a message from a man called Fraser. So, out of curiosity, I delved deeper into his profile. It read, 'Fraser - Tristar Entertainments.' There were plenty of newsfeed posts where he was putting calls out for models, actors, and musicians for films, music videos in exotic locations. It appeared that he was working with A list actors. In his newsfeeds he would mention famous models, big things brewing and exciting opportunities. With all of the things I read he seemed to be a real mover and shaker. He was highly active on there. I decided not to reply to his direct message.

Over the next couple of weeks, he persisted with his messages. He would tempt me by saying things like 'this was an amazing opportunity' and 'this was a once in a lifetime thing.' Still, I continued to ignore his messages because it all seemed too good to be true. The messages continued to flow.

One Saturday evening, Sarah and I were at home relaxing. We were chatting away when I decided to tell her about the messages I had been receiving. Sarah howled with laughter when she read the messages. She suggested that we google the company name. "Oh my God, Mum!" Sarah cried, "It's a film and entertainment company, and it's registered as a bona fide company based in America!" I laughed, but a part of me was intrigued. So, I decided that it was time to reply. My curiosity was peaked. I didn't think it could do any harm. So, I unlocked my settings and replied to his last message. When he replied he told me that his name was Fraser and he owned the entertainment company based in New York. He had several divisions throughout the States. He had a few satellite offices in the UK, as well. He wrote that he enjoyed directing films himself from time to time. He seemed to be incredibly well connected and vibrant, with a great sense of fun and humour. He was incredibly engaging.

During the following days, Fraser and I began to message back and forth. He often mentioned that he was looking for new talent and hinted that he wanted to make me a star. 'Yeah right, what a load of tosh,' I thought. I was enjoying his banter. I certainly didn't want, need, or expect to be a star; especially at my age. Though, he was so engaging and I really enjoyed 'chatting' to him. He was fun and goodness knows I needed some of that. Over the next couple of weeks, after our chats, I became hopeful for my future. He was so optimistic and seemed like a genuine bloke. We carried on messaging where he 'updated me' on his projects and business opportunities for me.

After a month or so, he began to request that I give him my mobile number. He said that he was bursting to hear my English 'accent.' He told me that he loved the English 'accent.' I was extremely reluctant at first. He told me that, from what he learned about me, he was certain that he could offer me a wonderful job working in the office based in London. When I told him that I was miles away from London, he suggested that I commute. He told me not to worry about it as I would be able to work from home, too. He said that if I was available, there would also be some travel abroad. This all seemed to be too good to be true, but he was extremely positive. I started to think about the job prospects. They sounded exciting and I definitely needed more money! I had never met anyone similar to Fraser before, apart from my dear work friend from years ago flamboyant Billy! Fraser told me that he was working on several projects at that time. There was a part of me that felt sceptical about the whole thing but I didn't know anything about the way Hollywood works so how would I know? I had often read articles in magazines about people being conned online. I had considered that those who allowed themselves to get drawn in by such con artists must be naive and gullible. Even though I was wary and cautious about sharing any of my personal information, there was something about Fraser. I don't know what it was, but I definitely wanted to explore this opportunity. I felt hopeful. I needed to find out more about him, and his business. After all, this could be a life changing offer.

After several weeks of regular messaging, we were becoming good friends. I felt that I had known Fraser for years. So, I thought it wouldn't do any harm for us to speak, at last! I was so excited at the prospect of hearing his voice. So, I decided to let him have my mobile number. Just as I had expected, he had a strong New

York accent and all the showbiz banter. He spoke at a million miles an hour, bursting with confidence. We must have talked for hours. He was so incredibly charming and engaging. So different from Donovan and Paul! He painted the picture that he really did have a fabulous business opportunity waiting for me. He was looking for someone exactly like me to run his business in London. I felt like I was being slowly absorbed into his world. It felt right. It felt good.

After a while Fraser joyfully announced that he was due to come to London on business. He planned to stay an extra couple of days. He asked if I would be available for his visit to Somerset. He wanted to chat more about the business. I was delighted and immediately said "Yes." He had arranged to fly to London the next week. He sent me his flight details and said that he would let me know when he arrived in London. We could then make arrangements to meet up in Somerset. We continued to talk until the night before his flight over to London. He told me that he would call me as soon as he landed in London, to let me know he was safe. I was thrilled at the prospect of meeting my new friend.

When I didn't hear from him for a few days, I became genuinely concerned. He had been relentless for weeks, now silence? I was worried that something had happened to him. He promised me that he would call when he landed. I checked the airlines and confirmed that his flight had landed safely. I called him, but his phone clicked straight to answerphone. I began to think that he was jet lagged or busy with his meetings. He told me that he did suffer horrendous jet lag. So, I was confident that he would call me when he could. He didn't.

A couple of days later, I was so relieved to finally hear from him. He was so apologetic. He had been busy in London with back to back meetings. He explained that he would need to stay there for a couple more days. He assured me though, that he would then hire a car to drive to Somerset. I asked him to let me know as soon as he knew his plans. I offered to book a local hotel for him, but he said his 'people' had that covered, and not to worry. He was positive that we would be meeting up very soon. I couldn't wait to meet him.

Eventually, he called me from his car. He was on his way to Somerset and expected to arrive in about five hours. He joked about getting used to driving on the 'wrong' side of the road and even pipped the horn to prove that he was on his way. He said that he was looking forward to seeing me. It felt to me as if I had already met him. I was so comfortable and relaxed with him.

After about four hours I called him. The phone went straight to answerphone. I assumed that his battery must have died. I waited anxiously to hear from him. It was about 2:00 am when finally, he called to say that he was lost. He was so tired that he had decided to pull over for a nap. He assured me that he would continue the journey first thing in the morning. I told him to stay safe and keep in touch. He said that he would and I went to bed.

The next morning, I didn't hear anything from him. I rang but he didn't pick up. I texted but nothing came back. I was seriously worried. I convinced myself that something awful had happened to him. I didn't hear anything from him all weekend. Eventually, around 2:00 pm on Monday afternoon, he rang me. He told me that he was back in the USA! What!? I was so disappointed. He told me that there had been a family emergency, soon after we had spoken on Friday. He said that he had no choice but to drive straight to the airport to catch the next flight home. He apologised profusely and explained that he hadn't been able to let me know. His phone had died completely and he had a problem with his charger. He was so apologetic. He seemed genuinely sorry. He repeated that there was absolutely nothing he could have done. He had no choice. He explained that his dad was seriously ill, and that was why he had to return to the USA, immediately.

He told me not to worry because he fully intended to come over again very soon. He needed to complete the business deal in London that he was busy negotiating. He promised me that we would meet the next time he was in London, no question. Part of me didn't believe him, though when I expressed my doubt, he quickly reassured me that I could trust him, implicitly and there was no reason to lie to me. We were friends so I believed him. I trusted that he wouldn't deceive me.

We continued chatting most days. We expanded our conversation and chatted about music, films, and anything and everything. I felt that he would be great to work for. We were so relaxed with each other, it was so easy to talk to him. He made me laugh and we seemed to have so much in common. It felt good to have a stimulating conversation with a man, especially after all the years of living with Paul, with his paranoid ways and suspicious mind. This guy seemed to be such a genuine person. I was becoming very fond of him. I respected and admired his intellect and his business acumen. He seemed to really respect me as well. So, the job in London would be perfect. It was going to be very well paid, and I knew I could do it. I was so pumped about it all.

Over the next 5 months we got to know each other incredibly well. We constantly bounced ideas off of each other. He made me feel joyful and confident. I hadn't felt like that, ever! It was towards the end of January 2011. Fraser told me that his next trip over to the UK wouldn't be for a while. So, he suggested that I fly over to meet with him. He assured me that if I booked the flight, he would pay me back as soon as I got there, as a business expense. I hated flying and I was reluctant to travel so far away from the UK but, I really wanted to meet with Fraser, and explore the business opportunities. I convinced myself that I could really benefit from a holiday, as well. That it would be good to get away for a bit.

I searched for flights and found a great return deal for 16-26 February. Fraser told me that he would be in Nashville when I was due to fly over so it would be best to book a flight there. When I checked, I noticed that it was even cheaper to fly there. So, I decided to go ahead and book the return flight for ten days. I had a couple of weeks holiday to take so I thought, 'Why not?' I had nothing to lose and it may turn out to be a fantastic opportunity. God knows, I deserved a holiday!

I decided not to tell anyone about my trip. I didn't want to invite awkward questions from Paul, mainly. I also knew that I would be back more or less before anyone realized that I had gone anywhere! I knew that Sarah would be fine on her own. Owen was going to be busy with Paul during that time and Tyler was busy with Minnie and the band. I didn't think there was any point in worrying anyone, I never went anywhere and I knew that people would think it was a weird thing for me to do. I decided that I would enjoy telling them all about my adventure once I returned in ten days. I relished the feeling of freedom and being allowed to do as I pleased, at last. After so many years of feeling trapped and the coercive behaviour by my ex-husbands, I felt the desire to disappear and be free. It was liberating!

The next day, I booked a ticket for the sleeper train to London, then an early flight the next morning. It was a nightmare journey on the sleeper train. I felt like I was in a coffin. There was no room to move. My bed was rock hard and I didn't sleep a wink. What a waste of money. I may as well have booked a normal seat as I would have been more comfortable. Fraser and I chatted on the phone most of the journey to London. He was really looking forward to seeing me and I couldn't wait to meet him either. This was my secret adventure! I was excited and optimistic about it. Fraser invited me to stay at his home. He had a guest room, especially for me. Everything was in place and I couldn't wait to get on the plane.

When I got to the check-in desk, the attendant asked me where I was going. I told her that I was meeting a friend in Nashville. She asked me for the address in Nashville. I suddenly realized that I hadn't asked Fraser for that. In all the excitement I didn't even think of that. The attendant warned me that, unless I had an address in Nashville and a return ticket, I may have problems getting through US Customs. They were hot on that sort of thing. I panicked and rang Fraser straightaway. I explained that I needed an address in Nashville. He gave me 'his' address. I was so relieved to get it.

Once again, Fraser told me he was looking forward to seeing me and reassured me that he would be at the airport to greet me. I suddenly became nervous. What if he didn't turn up? I would be stuck in Nashville on my own. What was I thinking? I began to wonder what I was doing. I boarded the plane.

CHAPTER 9

Hello Fraser, 2011

Jesus, that felt like the longest journey of my life. Most of it was spent being squashed up against the window by a huge, sweaty, fella who was seated next to me. Nightmare. I had never flown alone before. Along the way, I had convinced myself that I was going to be stranded in Nashville. To soothe my nerves, I decided that if that did happen, I would find a hotel, spend a few days there and be a 'tourist.' Afterwards I would fly back home and it would all have been an adventure. I told myself that everything would be fine. I had seen a couple of pictures of Fraser so I knew who to expect when I came through arrivals. What was I thinking? He was my friend. I knew he wouldn't let me down. Of course, I could trust him.

When I went through the Passport Control area, the attendant at Gatwick was proved right. Blimey! There were officers with guns all over the place. I instantly felt like a criminal. It was scary. I stood in line trying not to look 'suspicious,' which only made me feel even more so. The bloke in the kiosk had a kind face. He smiled and took my passport. He then asked me what the purpose of my visit was. I told him that I was visiting my friend for a few days. Fraser told me not to mention the business because I had a holiday Visa. He warned me that I may have problems if they thought I was there on business. The kiosk attendant asked me where I was staying. Thank God, I had the address, which I gave him. He then asked me what date I was travelling back to the UK. I showed him my return ticket and confirmed that I was flying home ten days later. As I took my passport back, he said, "Have a wonderful day," and ushered me through. Phew, I had made it. What a relief! Fraser advised me to bring plenty of clothes just in case I decided to stay longer. I told him, even though I always overpack, I fully intended to be flying home ten days later.

It was quite liberating being so far away on my own. I could be exactly who I wanted to be for the first time in my life. It felt good. I started to strut through to 'Arrivals,' even though I was really tired from the journey. As I came through the doors, I couldn't see anyone who looked like Fraser. Oh no! As the minutes went by, I became a bit nervous. Suddenly, this person bounded up behind me and tapped me on my shoulder. I turned around and was surprised to see a man standing there with his arms stretched out towards me. He was wearing a baseball cap, glasses, cream trousers, and a brown jacket. Not the attire I had expected at all, but he was friendly and delighted to see me. He gave me a huge hug, saying, "Hi baby, I'm Fraser, I'm very pleased to meet you!" 'Baby'? That was weird. Very American? Nobody had ever called me 'Baby' before. I had arrived apparently, in more ways than one! Thank God, the first hurdle was over. Now, I could relax and enjoy myself.

    I couldn't believe I was in Nashville. I loved the American accent. I felt like I was on a film set. Fraser took my suitcase and led me outside. I hadn't a clue where we were going or what we were going to do but after talking to Fraser for so many months I was confident I was in safe hands. There was a red pickup truck parked in the car park, or parking lot as they say over there. We walked towards it. There was a big bloke sitting in the driver's seat with a great big cowboy hat on. Everybody was wearing them. Of course, they were. This was Nashville. He jumped out of the truck and strolled on over to me, picked me up and squeezed me as if he had known me for ages. He introduced himself as Rett. He was Fraser's good friend. Fraser told me to 'hop in the front.' So, I shimmied along to sit in the middle, in between the two of them. I was nervously excited, even though I felt comfortable with them both. What have I got myself into? Fraser was very amused at my accent, which I thought was a bit strange after we had been chatting for five months. He seemed extremely over excited. He was quite loud and animated. I tried to mimic his accent, failing miserably. I don't do accents. Fraser and I continued to chat non-stop. Rett didn't talk much. Just as well as when he did speak, I couldn't understand a word he said. He had such a strong cowboy accent. I asked where we were going and Fraser didn't answer that. He said that he had been travelling quite a lot recently. Rett had only just picked him up, too. I had noticed that there was another suitcase in the truck. Rett said that he would drop us at the hotel. Fraser invited him to come back later and that we would all go out for some food.

I asked Fraser why we were not going to his home. He said that there had been a last minute change of plan. We would need to stay in a hotel for a couple of nights. He muttered that there was a slight problem with his house at the moment. When we arrived, I noticed that it was a sort of pleasant hotel, yet a bit kitsch. There were vases of plastic flowers on the cheap end tables and false rivers ran through the grounds with small wooden bridges over them. It looked like it had escaped from the seventies. We went to the front desk for Fraser to book our hotel rooms. The receptionist handed him the keys. When we got to what I thought was my room, Fraser barged past me, jumped on the sofa, and said, "It's ok, this is mine." What? I thought he had booked two rooms. I felt extremely uncomfortable and didn't know what to say. We made some tea, sat on the sofa, and talked for a while. At this stage I was getting tired. He had arranged for Rett to come back and take us somewhere for dinner. We met Rett in the Reception area. We didn't go far from the hotel as there was a diner close by. It was just like on the TV. A proper American diner.

I was really struggling to understand Rett. He had those cowboy eyes, just like Clint Eastwood. He squinted all the time and sounded like he had indigestion. It was as if he was holding back a huge burp. He seemed nice enough, though I kept catching him staring at me. It was as if Rett knew something I didn't. Right after we ordered our food, Fraser went off to take a phone call. He had done that a few times since we arrived at the hotel. He would walk away, stroll around, and speak very intensely into the phone. I couldn't hear what he was saying. I watched as he flapped his arms around and gestured while he was speaking. Fraser was quite animated and very much a New Yorker guy, at least what I had gathered from TV and films.

While Fraser was away from the table, Rett leaned across warning me to be careful. I wondered what he meant by that. When I asked him why, he just looked at me and said that I was a 'nice girl.' I found that a bit odd and disconcerting. Why say that? What did he mean by that? I giggled nervously instead of digging deeper. I told Rett that of course I would be careful.

Fraser drank spirits. After he had a couple of

those, he became loud and 'fun.' The alcohol seemed to hit him very quickly and he would become even more 'fun.' I really liked him. I thought I was in for a wonderful time. He was like a breath of fresh air. When we finished the meal, Fraser casually asked for the bill. When it arrived, he slid it in front of Rett. Rett looked really shocked, shook his head, muttered a swear word or two, then he slowly got up and went to the counter to pay. I didn't think much of it. I thought it was a bit odd and I offered to pay for my food. Fraser told me to put my money away as Rett would only insist that he pay.

Rett dropped us off in front of the hotel, saying that he would see us soon. We had a nightcap in the hotel bar. Fraser told the bartender to put our drinks on the room tab. After one drink we went up to the room. I was exhausted by this time so, I went into the bathroom, brushed my teeth, and hopped into bed. I fell asleep instantly. I assumed that Fraser had made himself comfortable on the sofa.

When I woke up the next day, I grabbed my robe and went into the living room. Fraser was already up, fully dressed and the blankets were folded on the sofa. He was busy texting frantically and smoking, which I didn't like very much. I asked him what we would be doing that day. He told me that Rett was coming to pick us up at lunchtime. We would be moving on to somewhere else. He didn't say where. I didn't ask as I didn't want to appear fussy, so I packed up and we went downstairs for breakfast.

The breakfast was enormous. They like their potatoes over there! There was far too much food for me. Fraser didn't eat a lot. He didn't seem to have much of an appetite. What a waste! After we nibbled at the breakfast, Fraser took yet another call and went outside. He was pacing around out there for what seemed like ages and talking frantically. When he came back, he told me it was 'business.' The bill came and Fraser just said, "Put it on the room."

We both went over to the reception desk to check out. Fraser stepped back slightly and looked at me. He cleared his throat awkwardly and asked if I wouldn't mind getting the bill. He was embarrassed to admit that he had left his wallet in Rett's car. He promised me that he would pay me back. I was taken completely off guard. 'Luckily,' I had a new credit card with me. So, I assured Fraser that it wouldn't be a problem. Fraser promised to pay me back as soon as possible. I didn't want to appear tight so I smiled and handed them my credit card. It was all a bit awkward.

Rett turned up, we hopped in and he drove us to a local bar. I was a bit mystified as I thought we would be talking business. Why were we at a bar? As it turned out we spent most of the afternoon there chatting and getting on famously when Fraser was not up and down on his phone and texting. He seemed to be terribly busy with his business. At a certain point, it started to get late. I began to wonder first of all when we were having dinner and where we were going to stay that night. I also wondered when the business meetings were planned. Fraser told me not to worry about business, as there was plenty of time for that. He said that he would sort somewhere for us to stay. He didn't want me to worry about anything, as it would all be fine. I needed to trust him, relax, and enjoy myself.

Fraser asked me if I wanted to experience the real Nashville. I wasn't sure what he meant, but I told him that I would, indeed. He told me that he had friends who lived close by. He described them as 'typical Nashville folks.' He was certain that they would invite us to stay with them for a couple of nights. I was nervous about this. I didn't know what to expect, but I didn't say anything. Rett dropped us off at Fraser's friends. Oh, my goodness, they lived in a trailer park. Oh God. There were run down trailers everywhere. It was like a gypsy camp. Suddenly, another huge cowboy bloke appeared out of nowhere and looked taken aback to see us. He just stood there, shaking his head. Fraser laughed as he walked towards him and said, "I bet you didn't expect this!" Turning to me, he said, "Meet Jed."

Jed picked me up, like Rett had the day before. He squeezed me so hard I felt something pop. I hoped he hadn't put one of my ribs out. It felt like it. Jed had an exceptionally long beard, wore dungarees and the obligatory cowboy hat. He invited us into his trailer. It was a right mess. It smelt musty. There was stuff everywhere. There were clothes strewn, a couple of dogs running around. Jed's wife, May, was drinking a beer on the sofa. She was tiny and skinny, with her long grey hair scraped back behind her ears in a ponytail. She only had one arm that worked. The other one was withered and looked like she had no use in it at all. It was either hanging next to her, or she put the hand in her pocket to keep it steady. She squinted at me and said, "Come in and sit down."

She swore a lot, and she had that strong southern accent, just like Rett's. Every other word she said was "fuck," though not in an aggressive way. It seemed natural and part of her vocabulary. She didn't look particularly pleased to see Fraser, though she was nice enough to me. Fraser went over and kissed her cheek. May looked him straight in the eye and asked him, "What the fuck are you doing back here and who the hell is this girl with you?" This was beyond awkward and I was baffled. Typically British, I kept on smiling and being over polite. May poured wine into a coffee cup and handed it to me. Or at least I hoped it was wine. It tasted like vinegar. Fraser was being his usual loud and bouncy self. He told them that we had come to stay for a couple of nights. I was shocked and not at all keen on this plan. Jed and May exchanged glances, as if we were the last thing they expected or needed. They looked back at us, smiled, and said that we were welcome. Clearly, we weren't.

There was a room at the back, behind a curtain we could use. Oh my God, when I looked in there, I saw a bed of sorts with old blankets and no sheets. What had I come to? May scared me. I thought she must be on something. She seemed like she was away with the fairies. She was staggering all over the place. Jed was drinking can after can of beer all evening. He must have finished off a crate at least. Fraser kept zooming in and out of the trailer to take numerous phone calls and his usual pacing around.

God knows how I managed to sleep that night. It must have been the jet lag. We managed to make a wall of pillows between us as there was only one bed. When I awoke Fraser was already up. They were all sober for the moment, sitting in the kitchen area and as soon as I walked in, I could sense an 'atmosphere.' They stopped talking when I joined them. Fraser had arranged for Rett to pick us up in an hour or so. When he arrived, he didn't come in. He sat in the truck waiting for us. Fraser told Jed and May that we would be back later, and that we would cook a nice meal for them. It was all extremely uncomfortable and surreal.

We jumped into Rett's pickup truck and he drove off. It was about lunchtime when we arrived at a karaoke bar. Oh, sweet lord, I couldn't believe it. The singing was incredible. The talent was outstanding. There was one girl who was amazing. After she sang Fraser went straight over to give her his number. He said that he wanted to be her manager. She looked straight at Fraser, unimpressed, and said, "Yeah, right!" She turned around and strutted away. She must have had loads of offers like that. She worked in a local supermarket and clearly didn't want to be a star, though God knows, she had the talent.

We stayed there for the afternoon. The guys enjoyed some more beers while I enjoyed coffee and the karaoke. I was absolutely gobsmacked at the standard of singing. We ended up having a great afternoon. I was enjoying the experience. I wanted to keep a clear head because I thought we would be talking business and having some meetings later that day. It became clear that I would be the one to initiate the talk about the business opportunities. So, three of four times when I started to talk about it to Fraser, he would look at his phone, and as he was walking outside say he had to 'deal with an important message.'

The music was great. It made me want to grab the microphone. I suggested this to Fraser but he said that we should be going back to the trailer park as he had promised to cook for us all. Without hesitation, he asked to borrow my credit card to settle the tab. I was shocked because he hadn't reimbursed me for the hotel yet. But, once again I didn't want to appear rude or tight. Still, I asked him why. He explained that he was going through a divorce, his finances were frozen for the time being, and until they had sorted things out, his funds weren't available. He apologised to me for putting me in such 'modest accommodations.' He explained that this was absolutely not his normal way. He had planned to have me stay at his lavish home and just as I was coming a number of aspects of his life went awry. He had been planning to give me the Royal treatment and knew that I expected that. So many deals were just about to come together and that's why he was so frantically on the phone. All of this would turn around really soon. He just kept painting this picture of how wealthy he was. He promised me that things would be settled soon, and that he would pay me back as well as cover the rest of my trip. I had my doubts, but we needed to pay the bill. I gave him my card.

We left the bar and went to the supermarket to buy food for the dinner he promised to cook. I didn't know that he had invited Rett to join us.

When we got to the check out, I was surprised as Rett appeared from nowhere. There was an uncomfortable silence, then Rett stepped in and paid for the groceries. On the way back to the trailer park, I asked Fraser when our meetings would be scheduled. I asked him about the London office. He jokingly, told me to stop with the questions and assured me that everything would become clear soon. I felt embarrassed as if I had stepped over the line.

When went to the Trailer park it was like Groundhogs Day as Jed was once more sitting in his chair guzzling beers and May was laid out on the sofa. They were hammered again. Eventually, Fraser cooked some food and we all sat outside to eat. Rett was noticeably quiet. He didn't join in much of the conversation and left shortly after the meal. I could tell that the conversation was stilted. There was some sort of problem between them all. I just didn't know what it was. It was late. I felt uncomfortable, so I went to bed.

The next day May said that she had some errands to run. She asked me if I wanted to go with her. Fraser looked slightly uncomfortable. He was clearly very unhappy about me going with her. I wanted to get out to see some of the place while I was there, so I jumped at the chance. While we were out, May told me that she had lost the use of her arm in a motorbike accident when she was a teenager. She drove an automatic car. She was used to driving with one arm. I was thinking that we were finally going sightseeing, but far from it. May was clearly delivering illegal drugs to people. We were out for about three hours. We drove all over the place visiting different trailer parks. She hardly spoke to any of her customers. She got out of the car, handed them a small package, took their money, stuffed it into her pocket and got back in the car.

Fraser was edgy by the time we got back. He told me that he had been worried about me and that we had been out for ages. He took me outside and asked me what we had been talking about. I told him that we were chit chatting about nothing really. He told me that I mustn't believe anything that May told me. He said that she was off her head on drugs most of the time. She didn't know what she was saying. I thought that was an odd thing for him to say about his friend, and I didn't know what he was talking about. He said that he had arranged for us to move on tomorrow to an apartment nearby. I was delighted to hear that. Thank God. I felt filthy in that trailer. I was desperate to get cleaned up. It was definitely not the holiday I had expected and was looking forward to the experience Fraser had promised me. What part of America was I seeing?

We said our 'goodbyes' to Jed and May the next morning. Once again, our chauffeur Rett turned up to collect us. This time though he seemed edgy and snappy. I could tell that he was feeling angry. Maybe it was because he was ferrying us around all the time. Once again, he was driving us to our new home.

I was disappointed when we got to the apartment. It was small, cramped and on the second floor of a large complex. Fraser said that he had covered the rent for a week because he was sure things would turn around by then. There wasn't a lot to see around the area. There was a huge Walmart Store across the road from us. The apartment was extremely basic. One room had a sink and a small cooker along the wall and a tiny shower room. We dragged our cases up the concrete stairs and settled in. That night there was a horrific storm. Tiles were flying off the rooftops and there was stuff flying all over the road. I was terrified. It was like the tornado scene in the Wizard of Oz. Fraser was still disappearing off to take calls in the pouring rain and wind, leaving me on my own. He didn't seem capable of standing still while he took calls. He was constantly texting, too. If I asked any questions about business that may pertain to me, he would get edgy and tell me to "stop worrying." I became leary of pressing the wrong buttons with him. I reminded him that I had my flight back in a couple of days so perhaps we can take some time to talk about the business. He said that we would talk about it tomorrow and confirmed that Rett would take me to the airport.

That night, Fraser told me that he had a soon to be ex-wife and a son who lived in Tennessee. He described her as 'the bitch from hell.' He said that because he had left her, she was bitter, twisted, and off her head. He admitted that she was one of the people texting him. She was being uncooperative about the divorce settlement. He was also trying to arrange to see his son. She had frozen the bank accounts but he would soon have plenty of money once they reached a settlement. She was supposed to have vacated his house with his son. She was refusing to let Fraser see him.

Fraser broke down. I felt so sorry for him. I know more than most the terrible heart ache of being separated from a child. He told me that he hated asking me to pay for things and remined me again that all would be rectified soon. I reminded him that I was going back shortly. That's when he mentioned that he wanted me to stay longer because he had several business meetings delayed until next week.

I hesitated, and before I could respond, he said that he was building his business and was certain that I would be a great asset. I asked him about his trip to London, my possible involvement there and his offices elsewhere. He said that there was a world of opportunity for me if I stayed a bit longer. I was convinced, hopeful and confused. There was a part of me that wanted to believe him and another part that wasn't buying it. I had grown very fond of him. He was so charming and charismatic. We had become good friends and I wanted to trust him. For a moment, I considered staying.

A couple of days later the flight was looming and I began thinking seriously about going back home. It was hard because I had begun to fall for Fraser. He was enchanting and funny. We got along so well and he was very protective of me. I felt that he knew me really well. He made me feel special and he listened to me. He was charismatic and I felt safe with him. He wasn't my type but I was beginning to find him attractive. There was just something about him. On the other hand, he had a vastly different way of life than I had expected, even though he promised me that this wasn't his normal way of life at all. Many of these aspects he didn't mention to me during our long phone chats when I was in the UK. At this point I felt that I needed to go back home, have a good think about things, and keep the relationship going long distance. When I told Fraser that I was going to keep my flight, he became really upset. He didn't want me to leave.

He assured me that once his divorce was settled, he would find us a house and that we could move in together. I reminded him that I had to think about my family, I felt that I couldn't just up and leave them, especially to America! I had Owen to consider, and Sarah and Tyler. This wasn't as easy as he made it all sound. He told me that he had fallen for me. He said that he didn't want to be without me and that I must stay with him. Even so, my gut feeling was telling me it was all too much, too soon, for me. I decided I would not be staying. I was certain that we would be able to sort something out but that I needed to go home. I started looking for my passport. I couldn't find it!

CHAPTER 10

Trust Me Baby - 2011

How on earth had I lost my passport? I don't lose things. I am extremely careful about stuff like that. I was positive that I safely zipped it in the inner compartment of my suitcase along with my return ticket as I always do. This didn't make any sense to me. I felt like I was going mad. I absolutely recalled putting it where I always put it and I checked for it often. I was desperately trying to make it 'appear' so that I could go home. I needed to apply for a replacement passport, and quick. All the while wondering what actually did happen to it. Fraser and I searched high and low for it. I researched and found that I could apply for a new one online when we had Wi-Fi. I spent a couple of hours panicking madly about it. Eventually, I accepted that I would have to stay a bit longer. Fraser suggested, "Maybe you could get an emergency passport. Don't worry baby, I will help you. Relax and enjoy yourself. You ain't going nowhere, baby." He looked delighted and gave me a broad smile as he lit up yet another cigarette and hovered in the doorway.

I was really concerned and I told Fraser that I needed to go home. I could see Fraser's face getting irritated, so I dropped the subject and hoped that I could get another passport as soon as possible. I convinced myself that I would be able to book another flight back before long. In the meantime, I had to find some courage to tell everyone where I was. How do I do that? I didn't want to worry anyone. After a couple of hours, I plucked up the courage to ring Mam. I struggled to hold back my tears as I explained that I was on holiday in the USA. She was shocked and asked me who I was with. I told her that I was safe. I said that I was with a male friend that I've known for a while. She asked, "Him? Who do you know in America?"

I panicked. Now she knew that I was with a bloke. I didn't know what to say to her. I told her that I hadn't much time as the call was expensive. I tried to reassure her that I was safe and that I was having a wonderful time, travelling around. I was about to tell her that we were in Nashville, but when I glanced over at Fraser, he was shaking his head and waving his arms around. He was slashing his hand across his throat urging me to end the call. I felt rushed and stressed. I told her that I would stay in touch, I was going to be staying in the US for longer than I had planned, and that everything was in order. I had a holiday Visa and I wanted to do a bit more sightseeing. At that point, I didn't know how long it would be before I replaced my passport. I felt that I had to convince everyone that I was having a wonderful time and that I had chosen to stay a bit longer. Mam agreed to let Dina and Harry know where I was and asked me if the kids knew my plans. I told her they didn't know yet and that I would call and let them know soon.

When I ended the call, I felt terrible. I hated lying to Mam. I wondered if she believed a word. Fraser had been listening to every word. He was standing over me so I felt under enormous pressure. Oh my God, I hated lying. I was desperate to tell my kids before they found out from somewhere else. Fraser seemed concerned about who I was texting. Whenever I made a call, he would stand next to me, listening hard to the conversation. I was completely unable to talk freely. Fraser had told me not to tell anyone where we were. He said that he didn't want his ex-wife to find out where he was. He said that she was troublesome and that she would make things difficult for us both. I couldn't understand why that was relevant to my family. He mentioned again that we needed to focus on our work and not deal with our families. This was 'the Hollywood Biz way.' The best process is to block everything else out and just focus, focus, focus. He reminded me again also that the projects were just about to pop, again 'the Hollywood Biz way.' I believed him at the time. I didn't know any better. His mention of the projects reminded me that I was still patiently waiting for the money Fraser owed me.

I was constantly thinking about Owen. So, regardless of what Fraser told me, I needed to call him to let him know where I was. When I rang the landline, Paul answered. I suddenly felt tearful when I heard his annoying voice. I didn't know what to say. I asked if everything was okay. Paul told me that our family friend Evangeline had come to stay with them for a few days, and that everything was fine. He asked me where I was. I told him that I had flown to the States for a holiday. He was stunned. For once I could tell he had no words! He immediately shouted to Evangeline, "You'll never guess where she is... bloody America!"

When I asked to speak to Owen, Paul said that he was too upset to talk to me. Owen had broken down when he heard Paul say that I was in America. I was furious. I told Paul that I wanted to be the one to tell Owen. I said that I could explain everything to him. Paul hadn't given me that chance. Fraser was standing right beside me signalling for me to give him the phone. He clearly wanted to speak to Paul. It felt like he wanted to take control of me, and the situation so he tried to grab the phone. I wasn't going to let that happen. No way. I moved away from him, waved him away, but he kept following me around the room.

Before I had chance to end the call, Fraser snatched the phone. He started going at it hammer and tongs with Paul. Fraser was effing and blinding at Paul. Where was this coming from. Fraser snarled, "You need to watch your back." This was a nightmare. What was Fraser doing and why? I could hear Paul shouting back at Fraser. He was trying to get a word in edgeways. There was no chance of that. Once Fraser got going, there was no stopping him. He was like a freight train. He didn't even stop to draw a breath. He wouldn't let Paul speak. I was frantic. This was not helping me at all. Paul would think that I had lost my mind. I was beginning to think I had. I was so incensed with Fraser for getting into my business, yet I remained contained on the outside because I didn't want to make it worse. All I could think about was Owen. Nothing else mattered at that point. I was desperate to talk to him. I was devastated. My heart was going like the clappers! What was going on with Fraser?

Eventually, after Fraser ran out of steam. He hung up on Paul and threw the phone on the bed. Unbelievable! I was dumbfounded, confused, angry and scared, all at the same time. I felt sick to my stomach and wanted to break things, including Fraser, but I knew I had to hold it together for self-preservation at this point. As Fraser nonchalantly swaggered out of the room for yet another cigarette, he said over his shoulder that he would be dealing with Paul from now on. I could barely speak. Is he that delusional that he thinks that is going to happen? I couldn't get my head around his delusion.

After a few minutes, Fraser calmly walked back in the room and was like a different person. He had a smile on his face like nothing had happened. He then assured me that everything would be fine and that honestly everything was fine. He switched from being completely unhinged to portraying himself as 'loving and caring' within minutes. He said that up until now I was not being supported in the way I deserved. He convinced me that he would take care of me. He told me that he loved me. He said that everything would be 'wonderful' if I just trusted him. He said that he would never lie to me.

All that being said I was still anxious about everything. This was all such a mess. Was I going to get paid back? How was I going to get home? How was I going to explain my absence from work to Philip? Fraser offered to email Philip on my behalf. He suggested that he could explain that I was on an extended holiday in America, and that I wasn't sure when I would be coming back. Oh no! That wasn't going to happen, although I would reach out to Philip in my own way. I had my home, career, and my family in the UK. I wouldn't just leave all that on a whim. Fraser then announced that, as far as he was concerned, I was working for him now. He decided that he wanted me to become a director of 'The Company.' Where did that come from? I thought that I was going to be running the office in London for him. Nothing had been discussed about me becoming a Director. Fraser then quickly changed the subject, reminding me that I should be concentrating on getting another passport, then he was talking about business. He was completely playing emotional 'ping pong' with me constantly.

After another anxious day, we went to the local bar. I had resigned myself to making the best of the situation, for the time being. Whenever we walked in the bars Fraser would immediately start working the room. He would 'Hi Five' people as he passed them as if he was some sort of celebrity. Maybe he thought he was, God knows. Everyone seemed to like him. He was extremely sociable and very engaging. People seemed drawn to him. He had charm and an aura of confidence. He played cards for money and was quite good at it. This particular evening, he won quite a bit of money. I broached the subject of reimbursement. He told me that he was keeping all of the receipts which would go through the business as expenses. He suggested that I do the same. I was keeping a record of all the expenses, as well so that I could keep track. He reminded me that I would be getting all my money back, with interest. Changing the subject once again, Fraser said that he would need to leave me at the bar for an hour or so as he had something to do. I stayed at the table and chatted with his friends. Everyone was interested in me because I was from England, or specifically London as they assumed. They got a kick out of my accent too.

As promised, after an hour. Fraser bounded back through the bar door and came straight to me with his arms wide open. I asked him where he had been. He smiled and said, "It doesn't matter where I have been, I have got something for you. Close your eyes." What was coming? When I opened my eyes, Fraser was standing in front of me holding a box. "Ta Dar!" he announced. Oh God. It looked like a ring box. Fraser was grinning from ear to ear as he told me to open it. It was indeed an engagement ring. I was speechless. Where on earth did he get that idea, and where did he get the ring? He was like the cat who got the cream. Strutting around in front of me.

I tried to speak but couldn't find any words. Fraser jumped up on the table and announced to the whole bar that we were engaged. He waved to the bartender to give everyone a drink to celebrate. Before I knew it, he had slipped the ring on my finger. For one thing, neither of us were divorced. How could we get engaged? For another thing, what? Fraser was on cloud nine. He was dancing around and swinging from girl to girl. He was over excited. He lifted my hand and whispered to me that he had 'made arrangements' for getting the ring.

An hour or so later, Rett walked into the bar and was surprised to see me because he thought that I had returned to England. I thought he knew that I had lost my passport. He shook his head and said that he hadn't a clue. I was sure that Fraser had asked Rett to search the truck for my passport. Fraser interrupted and announced to Rett that we were now engaged. Rett looked confused as he thought that I was going back to England. Fraser laughed and said that Rett must have forgotten that I had lost my passport. It seemed to me that Rett was mystified as to what Fraser was ever talking about, though he went along with it.

When we got back to the apartment, I decided that it was time to apply more pressure on Fraser to start paying me back. I had been picking up the tab for everything since I got there, some expenses without my knowledge. I asked him outright when I would be getting my money. I explained that my credit card balance was rising and I was concerned as to how I was going to pay it off. I was determined to get my money back. Fraser was edgy and began pacing around the room again. He said that he needed time to think. After a while Fraser said, "Baby, I've got a plan. I'll be able to pay off your credit card within the next week when we get you a new passport. We are going to New York." New York? I replied, in shock, "How the hell are we going to do that, and where are we going to stay when we get there? That's miles away." Fraser replied, "Don't worry, we can hire a car and take a road trip to New York. My sister, Danielle, lives in Staten Island. We can stay with her. I have already spoken to her and she is expecting us. I have a secret bank account in New York with loads of money in it. Nobody knows about the account, okay. Trust me baby, everything will be fine." I didn't know what to say. I was incredulous! New York? Secret bank account? Fraser continued, "I can pay you back straightaway, Baby. We'll have plenty of money to live on for a while. My wife isn't entitled to any of it." He gave me his best charming smile and a hug. I believed in him. I really wanted to believe him. I was in. Fraser could make anything seem reasonable. I wanted my money back and this seemed to be the way. Surely, he wouldn't lie to me.

CHAPTER 11

Hope & Promises

The next morning, Rett gave us a lift to the car hire place. Before we went into the office, Fraser asked me for my driving license. He explained that he would need to organise the car in my name. He was not able to drive in Nashville. He said that he had some driving offences on his record and that they wouldn't be able to lease a car to him. I panicked because I had an English license. I thought it wouldn't be valid in the States. "Trust me" Fraser said, I hadn't expected this but I reluctantly gave him my license. Everything went through okay, and the paperwork was all done.

I was keen to get to New York. I believed him about the money in the bank account. I was desperate to get my credit card paid off and my new passport. Fraser told me that we would hire the car for a week. Then we would return it in Staten Island when we got there. As it wasn't going to cost too much, and I knew that I was going to get all my money on the credit card back, I tried not to worry about it.

Despite the situation, I was excited about going to the Big Apple. I never imagined I would be able to go there. I had seen pictures in magazines, films and TV but never thought that I would be seeing it for myself. I had made a start on my passport application online, but every time I tried to continue with it, Fraser told me that he needed to use the computer for business. By the time I got back to it, the internet went down. It was a nightmare connection. Fraser told me to wait until we got to New York. He said that Danielle could help us with that. He put my mind at ease for the time being. I was convinced that we would get it sorted soon.

We loaded up the car and said our 'goodbyes' to Rett. Rett gave me a massive hug and wished me luck. He told me to take care of myself. I sensed that he was worried about me. What did he know that I didn't? I was excited and hopeful. The journey was going to take us over twenty hours so we would need to stop at a motel overnight. I felt like I was in a film. It was all so surreal. We went across the Blue Ridge Mountains of Virginia, which were actually blue! The scenery was amazing. We belted out songs by Michael Jackson most of the way. We had such fun together. When it grew dark, we stopped at a ridiculously cheap motel on the way.

When we drove into New York the next morning, I was amazed. The skyline was exactly how it looked on the television and in the opening sequences to many American films. The huge skyscrapers were overwhelming. I looked across to the Statue of Liberty and the Empire State Building. I was gobsmacked at how huge everything was. I immediately thought about the film Sleepless in Seattle when I gazed up at the Empire State Building. I felt so small in comparison. We drove through Manhattan and went over the Brooklyn Bridge. We headed straight to Staten Island to Danielle's house. I was totally overwhelmed with the city. I couldn't believe that I was there. It was like being beamed into a magazine feature. Fraser had a smug look on his face. He nodded his head as he watched me gawping at the grandiosity of it all. He seemed genuinely pleased to see me so excited. He showed a bit of his vulnerability.

While we were driving from Nashville, Fraser told me that Danielle lived modestly with her husband, Lionel and their three children. Gina was seventeen, Tori, fourteen, and Victor, twelve. Danielle was a registered child minder and looked after one child at home. Apart from that, she looked after the family. Lionel was a mail carrier and a heavy drinker. Fraser said that Lionel would take a crateful of beer with him on his daily rounds. They used electric postal vans and Lionel would have his cooler full of alcohol next to him while he did his round.

How Lionel could get away with that, I had no idea! Fraser warned me that Lionel could be a bit odd. He was noticeably quiet. He told me that I shouldn't take it personally. Gina the eldest was the favourite, without a doubt. Tori the middle one was a pleasant girl, overshadowed by her brother Victor, who was born with Downs Syndrome. They were an extremely well liked Brooklyn family with strong family values. Fraser told me a few tales about the rivalry between neighbourhood families. There had been many family feuds and arguments over the years. Certain families didn't speak to others and so on. I joked that it sounded like something off the Sopranos, or the Mafia. Fraser said that it was exactly like that. Fraser was deadly serious, which I found out later.

We were due to arrive at Danielle's house about 4:00 pm. On the way, Fraser warned me that Victor would get extremely loud and over excited when he saw him as he had Downs Syndrome. Fraser proudly told me his nephew loved to see him. He would get over emotional, I should prepare for that. We called by the liquor store, as they call the off-license shop over there. We picked up what looked like a gallon of sangria, and some beers. Fraser told me that Danielle loved sangria. I wanted to take a gift for them, so I didn't mind paying for it, even though my credit card was close to its limit by this time. Instead of going to the front door we went round the back of the house and into the kitchen. Danielle was standing in the kitchen and was startled. She clearly was not expecting us and was in total shock. Fraser assured me that she knew that we were coming. I would never show up somewhere unexpected, it's just not the way I work. Danielle blurted out, "What the fuck are you doing here and who is that?"

Immediately after that, she looked at me and apologized. Fraser burst out laughing and gave her a massive hug. She peered beyond him, and straight at me. I could tell that she was speechless and asked again who I was. Fraser told her that I was his girlfriend from London. I thought that was weird. He had been introducing me as his wife to everyone else we met!

Danielle gave me a hug and said that she was pleased to meet me. She was a real New Yorker just like Fraser and I liked her straightaway. She was warm and had a kind aura about her. I knew we were going to get on well. I finally felt comfortable, and it was good to be in her home. Victor was upstairs with Tori. Fraser said that he wanted to surprise him so, he disappeared upstairs. As I expected, Victor went nuts when he saw Fraser. What a racket! He was a heavy child. He thumped around upstairs, screeching with delight. Fraser loved the attention and he lapped it up.

Danielle turned to me, inviting me to take a seat. She opened the sangria and got the special wine glasses out for us. She told me I was her honoured guest. We instantly got along. She spoke a million miles an hour in a wonderful New York accent. I loved listening to her. She asked me where I was from again. I tried to explain, though I knew she didn't have a clue where Somerset was. I got the impression she wanted to ask more questions, yet she was holding back. I told her that I had three kids and that I was going through a divorce. Fraser came zooming back downstairs with Victor and Tori. We all chatted around the table. They obviously had a lot to catch up on. Despite that I sensed an awkwardness, an atmosphere. Danielle would start to say something and then stop herself and say, "I can't." I didn't understand. I thought that must be the way they speak!

After a while Danielle asked us where we were staying. I didn't know what to say and looked at Fraser. He looked uncomfortable, cocked his head, and smiled at Danielle. She shook her head and looked quite uncomfortable. She said that we were welcome to stay in the basement for one night. Fraser assured her that we would find a hotel the following day. Danielle had noticed the car parked outside and asked if it was ours. I told her it was a hire car. She asked me whose name it was under. I told her it was mine. Another knowing smile came over her face and she turned away grinning to herself and almost laughing. What did she know that I didn't?

CHAPTER 12

Spinning Yarns

Lionel stumbled through the door from work about 4:00 pm that same day. He was absolutely hammered. His nose was a mixture of red and blue. He was stunned to see us. He glared at Fraser, then at Danielle, then me, back at Fraser and shook his head. He looked furious. Danielle gave him a knowing look and a long stare, so he didn't say a word. He just disappeared into the backyard. He sat on a bench drinking beer for the next couple of hours while Danielle made dinner. When she called him to join us, he had fallen asleep on the bench. Though, I thought it was weird behaviour of Lionel, everyone else seemed to accept it.

After dinner, we played cards. Lionel joined in for a while. It was clear to me that he had a problem with Fraser. He was so drunk by 10:00 pm that he went to bed. Danielle enjoyed a drink, too, yet it didn't seem to affect her. I was very tired so I told Fraser I wanted to go to bed. I didn't want to be involved in the drinking, so we went down to the basement. It was full of clutter. There was a large TV on the wall, with a corner sofa opposite it. We rearranged the cushions to make a bed. We lay there for a while, watching anything and everything on the TV. Fraser seemed to need the television on when we went to bed. That kept me awake but he seemed to need the noise around him. He appeared to be hyperactive and constantly wanting stimulation. I was beginning to think that he had a sleeping disorder. To add to that he was constantly calculating his next move, problem solving and strategizing. He just couldn't seem to switch off and relax.

I mentioned to Fraser that I had noticed that Danielle seemed surprised to see us. He just said off the cuff that 'she must have forgotten our conversation.' He told me that they spoke regularly, even though they hadn't seen each other for a couple of years. I observed that Danielle seemed to be incredibly careful with her words. I had a feeling that there was something going on between them. I must have been overtired because I couldn't sleep. At around 2:00 am Fraser made some tea for us and we talked. I told him that I had sensed that there was a problem between them all. Reluctantly, Fraser admitted that he and Lionel got into a fistfight a few years ago because Danielle had lent $20,000 to Fraser, without telling Lionel. He explained that he had needed the money to pay for some work on the roof of his house in Tennessee. Fraser assured me that he had paid them every penny back, with interest. I was suspicious that Fraser actually hadn't paid them back. He assured me that Lionel was overreacting. He was so convincing.

When I woke up the next morning I came up to the kitchen. Danielle was there making coffee and breakfast. The kids had all gone to school. Fraser was outside having a cigarette. While Danielle and I sat at the kitchen table, she asked me what our plan was. I told her that I wasn't completely clear what Fraser had arranged. He has many irons in the fire. I didn't want to share with her that we were actually there to access Fraser's secret bank account. As soon as I got my money and passport, I intended to fly home.

She asked me how we met and how much I knew about Fraser. I filled her in on the basics and said that I knew he was going through a divorce. She confirmed that indeed it was a messy divorce. I asked Danielle to tell me more about Fraser. She told me that he and his wife owned a house in Tennessee. His wife was living there with their young son. Danielle thought that she had kicked Fraser out. She told me that they had a very volatile relationship and that they fell out often, usually because Fraser wasn't working. Alarm bells rang. I kept quiet and listened to Danielle filling me in on Fraser. She told me that Fraser was taking a huge risk being in New York. She said that he was breaching his child support agreement so, he wasn't supposed to leave Tennessee. She said that if his wife knew that he was in New York, she could report him to the authorities. She told me that he could be arrested and taken back to Tennessee. What? That explained why he didn't want anyone to know where we were. This made me extremely nervous. What on earth was going on? I decided to confront Fraser, and quick.

Danielle said that Fraser's wife had contacted her trying to find him and that Fraser had been sending her vile messages. He was threatening her and telling her that he would be back to take their son. He told her that she was an unfit mother and that she was unstable. Danielle said that she was worried about Fraser leaving Tennessee. I was so confused. This was all new to me. Fraser had assured me that it was an amicable split. He said that his wife had reconsidered and was desperate to get him back. He explained that this was why she was constantly texting him. He made it clear that he didn't love her, and that he had no intention of going back to her, no matter how much she pleaded with him. What?

My head was spinning with all this other side of the story. Which one was true? I wanted Fraser to be true but what if Danielle's story was the truth? This wave of panic overwhelmed me. My heart was pounding, my hands were clammy, my stomach was churning and I began to question everything. Before I could find out anymore from Danielle, Fraser came into the kitchen and informed Danielle that we would need to stay a few more days. After that, he would book a hotel. It was all very awkward. I could tell that Danielle didn't want us to stay but felt that she couldn't refuse her brother. Though, she did mention that Lionel wasn't comfortable with the arrangement, Fraser reassured her that it would only be for a couple more days. He said that he really wanted to show me New York and that it would be easier if we stayed with them. She agreed.

There were so many uncomfortable silences and 'expressive' looks going on around me, I was getting dizzy! I couldn't help but wonder what was going on with these people. I'd never met anyone like them. This was way out of my comfort zone. Even though I have experienced my fair share of family dynamics this was off the scale. I decided that it was none of my business and that I would keep the 'bleep' out of it! I had shared with Danielle that I had lost my passport. She seemed genuinely concerned and suggested that she could help me apply for another one. I thanked her and told her that Fraser had already started the application. He said that once we had a better Wi-Fi connection that would hasten the application process. It had been difficult to stay connected while we were travelling. I told Danielle that my holiday Visa was valid for three months and assumed that I could get a replacement passport soon.

I just wasn't comfortable with this family chess game and all the 'if's,' 'but's' and 'maybe's.'

Later that day, Fraser and I were in the back yard when I decided to confront him about what Danielle had told me. He completely spun it like the most skilled politician. He discredited Danielle. He gave me every reason to doubt Danielle and no reason to doubt him. He reminded me that his divorce would be settled very soon and that he was looking for a house and he was really concentrating hard on the business, whether I saw it or not. He told me that there was so much going on behind the scenes. He promised me that we would be flying back and forth to the UK regularly and that we were partners now. From the way he was painting the picture of our future, I had absolutely no reason to doubt him. I was extremely excited for our future together. I was captivated and mesmerised by his confident manner. He kept explaining to me how things work in America. He knew that I was a blank canvas and that I didn't know better. I didn't use Google then so researching American laws didn't occur to me.

The next day we were off on our sightseeing trip. We caught the early ferry from Staten Island into Manhattan. It was amazing. We passed the Statue of Liberty on the ferry. We walked to Times Square from the ferry station. We wandered all through Central Park and then past the Empire State Building. We stopped for some street pretzels and other vendor food. We walked down Wall Street and looked up at the skyscrapers that blocked the sky, and the famous bull. By 6:00 pm we finished at Ground Zero. It was twilight and there was a warm wind was rising. I was moved by the silence even though there were construction vehicles and workers everywhere. It was awful. I could feel so many lives lost and spirits in the air. I felt honoured to be there. It was incredibly sad and I took a moment to remember all those who perished on that dreadful day. To think so many people woke up to a normal day but never came home was unthinkable. A piece of my heart will stay there.

The next day as usual, Fraser was constantly on his phone. He announced that he needed a new one. I wanted an American phone, too. So, we spent that day in a mobile phone shop. Almost immediately, Fraser befriended the man in the shop. He was so personable and engaging. He was hysterically funny, too. He negotiated heavily to get us the best deal that he could. He was incredibly clever. He talked fast, changed from subject to subject so that people became confused, quickly. By the end of the day, Fraser had secured a great 'family plan' for both of us. He guaranteed that this expense would be charged through the business.

A couple of nights later, while I was in the basement, I heard Fraser talking to someone upstairs. I couldn't help listening to him. Everyone else had gone to bed. He was becoming increasingly irate and angry. He sounded like he was trying to convince somebody that he was in Tennessee. He was telling them that he knew that there was a specific car parked on the roadside near the house. He was saying that a house further down the road was lit with their porch light. He was even saying that he could see someone that he knew walking down the street. He kept asking the caller how he would know all this if he was not there. After a while he seemed to convince the caller, that he was not lying! He calmed down and told them that he would speak to them the next day. When he came downstairs, he was laughing and rubbing his hands together and muttering "silly fuck," under his breath.

Then Fraser noticed that I was still awake. He asked me if I had heard his conversation. I said that I couldn't help but overhear. He seemed agitated but assured me that all was well. After a while he admitted that he shouldn't have left Tennessee. He explained that he was on his Google Maps app searching the streets and the houses in his Tennessee neighbourhood, because he needed to convince his wife that he was still there. He thought it was hilarious that he tricked her. During our many late night conversations, Fraser mentioned that he had also been looking for a house in Brooklyn. He said that we would view a couple the next day.

CHAPTER 13

Expensive Perfume and Designer Shades

A few days later, Fraser came into the lounge looking like a country gentleman all dressed up. He had on English tweeds, a crisp white shirt, and a brown plaid Yorkshireman's flat cap with brown brogues. He told me to get dolled up because we were going to the races! So, I did. When we arrived at Belmont Park, Fraser was like an excited kid at the fair. He was certain that we would win loads of cash. I couldn't help but chuckle to myself. I was excited at the prospect and thought it would be a bit of fun, too. We often had so much fun together. As we wandered through the park, I felt like I was transported back in a time machine to my teenage years. The first place we went was to view the horses in the paddock. It was wonderful to be around the beautiful horses, again. I was immediately transported back to my riding days. I fondly remembered my first love, the event horse Gorgeous Grey.

Fraser was strutting around like he owned the place but he was clearly uncomfortable. Unlike me, he was visibly scared of the horses so he ushered me to the bar to get away from them. We sat at the bar and ordered a coffee, when an old man came to sit next to us. Of course, Fraser's face lit up and he immediately introduced us both, me as his wife! I wasn't prepared for that! The man introduced himself, as Mitch. He explained that he was a good friend with Joss, one of the only female jockeys around at the time. He felt that she hadn't had much luck lately and that there was a clear bias against her. Fraser started asking probing questions of Mitch about Joss. Soon he persuaded Mitch to ask Joss if she would meet with us. Fraser confided in Mitch that we would be able to help promote her.

While Mitch went off to chat with Joss, Fraser told me to go along with whatever he said. After about an hour this tiny woman appeared, alongside Mitch. She was the size of an 8-year-old and she seemed really shy. Fraser was very convincing of his abilities to promote her. For a small $500 retainer, we could make Joss a star. Joss seemed delighted and said that she was definitely interested. I was noticing that there seemed to be no end to Fraser's ability to be versatile. It appeared that he seamlessly moved from movie mogul to jockey promotor within an instant. This man had talent or so it seemed to me because I didn't know any better. I was delighted to be taken back into the wonderful world of horses, too. Even after so many years the feeling of that time in my life came back.

The whole environment transported me right back to my happy place.

When we returned to the house, Fraser couldn't wait to tell Danielle about managing Joss. He was so excited at the prospect of spending more time at Belmont Park for a while. That night Fraser put together a contract for Joss. It was a standard contract that he had used before but he adapted it for Joss. The next day, Joss signed the contract without hesitation. She became our first client.

Now to my delight we were spending our time at Belmont Park. Everyday we would meet with the trainers. We went to the stables and watched the grooms tending to the horses. The magnificent animals took my breath away and brought back some of my most beautiful memories while I watched the trainers timing them at the gallops. I absolutely loved being part of this wonderful, exciting world again. It reminded me of when I was a teenager and all those special and happy times being in the stables. I loved the smell of the leather saddle soap in the tack rooms. Those many hours I spent mucking out the horses and plaiting their manes and tails for the shows were magical. Those wild days of catching the ponies and riding fearlessly bareback across the fields in the early morning were exhilarating. All the cross country and show jumping competitions I competed in and the glorious feelings I had when I won a rosette; I will never forget. Being at Belmont brought back so many happy memories for me. Even though I was across the pond, I felt so at home at Belmont. It was my little piece of home.

I was part of the glamorous side of the horse world. The atmosphere was filled with expensive perfume and cologne in the fancy restaurants. We enjoyed dining in the exclusive clubs. The couture dresses and hats the ladies wore were stunning; not to mention the Armani suits and the slick sunglasses of the gents. Now that Fraser and I were being considered promotors we were allowed access to all areas. We would spend time in the boxes and the members enclosure. I felt swept away with the romance and was getting closer to Fraser every day. This was the life. It suited us both and I was falling deeper for Fraser. We were so invested in each other emotionally and physically by now. We were becoming well known as the cool American businessman and his English wife.

Because we were really focussing on getting Joss's promotion up and running and I was reliving the best memories of my life, I wasn't paying attention to the other aspects of me being in America. I wasn't tracking my passport application. Fraser was supposed to be dealing with that anyway. I wasn't checking with Fraser about reimbursement and we weren't chatting about the business opportunities in London and elsewhere.

Out of the blue alarm bells rang again, and I came back to earth. I realised that I needed to deal with my American logistics. When I broached the passport subject with Fraser, he said that he had completed the application and we needed to wait until it was processed which should be 'any day now.' Because I realised that I most probably would be leaving soon, the conversation about my role in the London office needed to happen. So, I reminded Fraser that we should strategize about it. He said that he 'completely agreed,' he absolutely wanted to do that but then he redirected me yet again by insisting that 'our first priority was Joss right now.' So, I was confident that we would deal with it soon. I realised at this stage that I needed to keep on top of these things. I couldn't leave it to Fraser.

CHAPTER 14

My Ticket Back to Reality

One day when we arrived back from Belmont, Danielle came dashing over to me, wielding something in her hand. Oh my God! She was holding my passport! I couldn't believe it. I was astounded and asked her where she had found it. She told me that she was sweeping the wooden floor in the lounge, when it dropped out of the sofa. What the hell?? I instantly turned to Fraser with incredulity. He just stared at me. He appeared to be speechless, for once. I couldn't find any words, either. I was so puzzled and asked of no-one in particular, "How could it have got there?" I was stunned. Fraser didn't reply to anything I said. He just shook his head. Danielle suggested that it must've fallen out of my handbag. I was certain that it hadn't as I hadn't seen it since we left Nashville where I had dumped everything out and searched high and low for it. I looked in every pocket in every part of all of my luggage. There was only one explanation for this. Fraser must have hidden it when I was due to fly home. He must have taken it out of my case when we were in Nashville. When we arrived at Danielle's house, he must have hidden it in the sofa. What the hell?? I didn't want to accept that he would do such a thing. I realized that he didn't want me to leave, but it never occurred to me that Fraser would go to such lengths to stop me. It never occurred to me that he would ever manipulate me. I mean he even helped me to look for it!

It's as if at this moment I woke up. I moved through the emotions of feeling incredulous, angry, and betrayed within seconds. Now it was time to go home. The crushing reality was that I needed to cut my losses and let go of this fantasy, this dream. For some reason having my passport in my hand felt literally like my ticket back to reality, and home. I felt for the first time in weeks that I could change my game.

Next stop on this incredible journey was to get my money back so I could buy my ticket home. When I confronted Fraser about the passport, he had the audacity to deny it. When I reminded him of the money he owed me, he became instantly irritated and tried to redirect me, but I wouldn't have it. I really pressed him for my money. Big mistake! Fraser quickly leapt on top of me. He put both his hands around my throat. He was furious and started yelling at me. He was telling me that I had no right to demand my money back. I was fighting to get him off me. I was terrified. I was frantically trying to release his grip around my throat.

Danielle heard the commotion and hurried downstairs, instantly pulling him off me. She slapped him hard across his face and screamed,

"Fuck off and get out of my house." Fraser was seething and screaming profanities as he stumbled out of the house. I was shocked and burst into tears. Danielle hugged me. She recommended that I should think about going home. Yeah really?? I explained to her that I had no money available to me because her brother had cleared my bank account and that my credit card was maxed. I didn't have access to any other money. Danielle said, "He's my brother and I love him but you need to get out of here. You need to go home." Danielle was ashamed of him. She was furious with him. We both were.

After about thirty minutes, Fraser strolled back in the house, as if nothing had happened. He came springing through the door, proclaiming that he had spoken to Richie, his friend. Fraser explained that Richie worked at Fraser's bank in New York. He arranged a meeting with Richie the next day to collect a large sum of money owed to him. Before I had a chance, Danielle asked Fraser, "What money?" Fraser explained that this was a payment due to him for work he had done a while ago. He confirmed that this was a substantial amount. Danielle and I glanced at each other. We both hoped that this was true.

Danielle questioned Fraser about my bank account, and credit card. He looked uncomfortable, but immediately defended himself, and assured us that there was no need to worry about either. He joked that I had been very generous, he said that I enjoyed spending my money and that I would be paid back tomorrow. He lied and said that I had offered to pay for things. He was like a kid at a party. Darting around and making jokes. I was still spinning from his attack. I didn't know what to think. One way or another, I had managed to scrape through another day in 'paradise.' I felt like I was riding an emotional roller coaster. One minute I was worried about our next steps, the next, Fraser was bragging that everything was going to be alright. For weeks I'd felt baffled and didn't know what to think anymore.

The next morning at 9:00 am we had an appointment with Richie at the bank. As we set off to the city, Fraser seemed cocksure of himself. He said that he couldn't wait to pay off my credit card that very afternoon. He would do the transfer while he was at the bank. At last! I was eager to book my flight home.

At 9:00 am on the dot, we drove up to the front door of the grand American bank with big marble pillars at each side of the door. Fraser excitedly leapt out of the car. I grabbed my bag and started to join him. Fraser was heading toward the door when he said over his shoulder, "Baby, park the car for us. I'll be as quick as possible. Make sure you don't get a ticket. "I'll be right back." I was surprised that I wasn't going in, but it was okay with me. I hoped to God that he would be back with all the cash. I was anxious but believed that this was happening.

I waited anxiously for forty-five minutes. Fraser came storming back towards the car. I realized instantly that there was a problem. I was right. Richie hadn't turned up. Fraser was beyond furious, and so was I, but I had to keep it together. He said that there was nothing he could do without Richie. I started to shake, with fear and anger. I was so disillusioned; my heart sank. I stayed silent. Fraser began to swear. He was slamming his hand on the steering wheel, screaming, "Fuck, fuck, fuck... I will kill him. I will break his fucking legs. I want my money."

We were still in the car park when Fraser called Richie over and over again. Eventually, Richie answered. Fraser laid into him. He lost it completely and went ballistic. He threatened Richie that if he didn't get here within the hour, he would arrange to have his legs broken, or even worse 'he was a dead man.' His tirade of abuse was unrelenting. He crashed the phone down on the floor of the car and announced that we would wait for just one hour. Fraser reclined his seat, laid back, and pulled his cap down over his eyes. I was rigid with fear. I needed to scream, or cry, or both. After 45 silent minutes, Fraser went into the bank. It wasn't long before he was running back towards the car. He was flushed and infuriated. He slumped down in the seat and mumbled that there was no sign of Richie. I wanted to cry; I didn't dare! I was barely breathing when Fraser started the car. As we drove out of the city towards Staten Island, I fell into a daze. I couldn't even be bothered to think anymore. I hadn't a clue what to do next. I felt so stuck.

As we drove, the silence was deafening. All I could think about was my money, and my flight home. After a while I dared to ask Fraser if we had an alternative plan. All at once he stopped the car, he started choking me with his left hand and forced my head hard against the headrest. He was screaming into my face, "Stop asking questions." Fraser was at breaking point. I grabbed his hand and struggled to push him off me. Finally, he freed me and I took a huge gasp. I was petrified but kept my silence. He began thumping his hand on the steering wheel, yet again. He warned me to keep quiet as he needed to think. I couldn't speak anyway. I was frozen to the seat. Then we seemed to drive around for ages, in silence. I hardly dared to move.

As soon as we walked into Danielle's door, she realized that we hadn't got the money. Fraser didn't say a word. He marched straight passed her and outside for a smoke. She asked me what had happened. I told her that Richie hadn't turned up. She looked me straight in the eye, and said, "There is no Richie, there is no account. Fraser is lying." I had nothing left; no tears, no words, nothing. I sat at the table in a daze. How could all this be a lie? I just couldn't comprehend. I had heard Fraser on the phone countless times to 'Richie.' Danielle assured me that he didn't know anyone called Richie so he was obviously talking to someone else. God only knows. I didn't know what the truth was, and what was a lie. I felt that all my hopes of getting home were in pieces.

A couple of hours later we managed to all be sitting around the dining table somehow, when Danielle mentioned that she organised a charity event every year for the Special Olympics. Fraser was listening intently. I could see his head filling with ideas. He thought that we could organise a race at Belmont, for the Special Olympics, too. We could host a garden party in the hospitality area. It would be an amazing event, for an amazing cause. Fraser was certain that we would raise loads of money for the cause. Danielle and I were dubious about it but Fraser became animated and excited with lots of ideas. So, we started planning the event.

Fraser was on a mission. He immediately began to talk to almost everyone at Belmont Park about the event. Before we could catch our breath, Fraser had arranged to see the PR lady and managed to secure part of the hospitality area. He explained to her that we were having numerous different stalls, and there would be a couple of celebrity appearances throughout the day, as well as face painting and afternoon tea, and, of course, a bar. What?? Fraser had broken my trust when he attacked me. I was trapped, for the time being. I had seen another side to Fraser. I realized that I had to keep Fraser calm, and go along with his plans, in the hope that I would get enough money to fly home, soon. I felt that right now, this was a waiting game, for me. I was beginning to become an Oscar deserving actor.

We started creating flyers and invited Joss to present a short talk about her life as a jockey. Of course, she would be competing in the race, too. Fraser informed everyone that there would be charity collection boxes placed everywhere. Everyone would be able to donate to the cause. Fraser coolly announced to me that his plan would be to pick up the charity boxes at the end of the day and take the money. I was horrified. No way! That's stealing from a charity. I felt that I couldn't be any part of that. Fraser laughed and told me to relax. Fraser was like the ringmaster of a circus, orchestrating the show.

Danielle was worried about the event. She repeatedly emphasized to Fraser that she would never forgive him if anything went wrong with this event. She was concerned that it would be her reputation at risk, not his. Fraser was a hundred percent certain that it was all going to go like clockwork. He was on the phone 24/7, talking to the agents for the celebrity appearances, preparing for the face painting and side stalls. He was persistent and seemed determined to make this work for all of us.

On the day of the event, Fraser seemed to be disappearing. He left me to run the event, the best I could. People started asking me who the personalities were. Of course, I didn't know. Fraser wouldn't even tell me. He would only confirm that they were 'mystery' and high profile guests. He bragged that one of them was an extra on the US TV show, 'The Sopranos,' and that he was Fraser's friend. I had to bluff my way through the whole event. It was exhausting. Meanwhile, Fraser was switching from excitement to animated and back again. He appeared just in time to watch Joss present her talk in the marquee. Oh dear, it went down like a lead balloon. It was dreadful. She didn't seem to have any idea how to present herself; she seemed unprepared. Everyone quickly lost interest and dispersed outside. Joss was fuming. She bolted straight over to Fraser and tore a strip off him, then marched away.

The anticipation of the attendees about the celebrities was becoming unmanageable. The PR woman appeared and demanded to know who was coming and when. Just as Fraser was wavering, his phone rang. He walked away to take the call. I was left with her, feeling incredibly awkward. Fraser became even more lively, he was hurling his arms around as he talked. When he returned, he looked a bit sheepish when he told us that the celebrities were delayed, and that they had to go straight on to their next appearance. In other words, they were bailing on us, if there ever were any to begin with. I was humiliated. The PR woman lost her temper. She told Fraser that he was incompetent, and that he had humiliated her as well as the Park. She ordered us to leave right then, and never to return. Fraser furiously said, "Calm the fuck down." She rolled her eyes and strutted away. Fraser bolted to the bar and left me to pick up the pieces of this almighty mess.

Everything seemed to be falling to pieces. People were leaving in droves. Danielle was furious and left. Mitch came to me demanding that I gave him his $600 that we owed him. I told him that it was Fraser's deal and he was at the bar. I looked over to see Fraser rambling to Mitch. I could see that Mitch was outraged and could overhear him yelling that we were con artists and that we were deceiving everyone. I heard him yelling that he researched us and found that not one person had ever heard of us. Jesus Christ; they thought both of us were fakes. I rushed to the bathroom and erupted into tears. I was terrified. I must have hidden in the bathroom for ages, pondering about what to do. Eventually, I summoned enough courage to return to the marquee. I decided that I had to deal with this situation head on.

When I strode into the marquee, Fraser was perched on the side of the stage, alone. I asked him if he had collected the charity boxes. He said that he certainly had, but they were all empty. Not a single person had donated anything. We were broke. We must hand in our Belmont passes at the gate on our way out of the park. The management had ordered the security men not to allow us back in. Because we had blown it with Danielle, she told Fraser before she left the park that beyond question, we had to collect our belongings and leave. She said that she was finished. I froze. We had no money, no income, nowhere to go and a car that was on lease. I was convinced that Fraser wasn't paying for that either. As it had Nashville plates, I felt that we would be noticed soon. We were on the run. The whole shebang had gone pear shaped, again. I was afraid to be alone with Fraser although I knew that I had to keep him calm or else I was going to be in danger.

When we arrived at Danielle's house, I went downstairs straight away to get my belongings together. I was furious, humiliated, disappointed, and worried. Fraser suggested that I take my time as he was going to try to secure us one more night. Somehow, he achieved it. The next morning, Fraser told me that he had arranged for us to go to his parents in Brooklyn. After a couple of uncomfortable days with his parents we had to leave. They obviously didn't want us there either.

At this stage we had nowhere to go. We drove around pointlessly for hours while Fraser kept very silent. We were running out of gas and we couldn't go back to Belmont. We drove around until it was dark. We pulled into an empty car park and attempted to sleep, bolt upright in the car. It was impossible, I was unable to sleep for longer than about ten minutes at a time. I was cold, hungry, and desperate to lie down. We repeated this nightmare for the next few nights. I was exhausted and tearful. We managed to use the bathrooms at a local diner we frequented. Fraser became friendly with the staff and would order coffees and such, and I would use the bathroom to freshen up. Even so, I felt dirty all the time. My hair was a mess. I felt so scruffy.

Fraser knew we couldn't continue living this way. He was troubled and short tempered. I didn't have the guts to ask questions. Even though I desperately wanted to call home for help, I was petrified that he would really hurt me. I also felt that he wanted to take care of me. It did appear that he was working on our next steps. Numerous times during the day he would park the car and get out to make and receive calls. Even while he was driving, he was constantly texting. I was praying that something was going to happen; that something would come true. He told me that he was busy making plans, working on deals and the business. I felt that he wanted to take care of me, but the stress was getting to him. He appeared quite calm while we were driving around, one day. So, I took up the chance to ask him if he had a plan. He immediately hit the roof, he began to swear and shout at me. The car was veering all over the road, again. He was losing it. I was rigid with fear. He repeatedly told me to stop whingeing. He said that I was turning out to be a nuisance and he suggested that I go back to England. Before I had a chance to respond, he stopped the car on the side of the parkway and told me to clear out. I just stared at him. I daren't speak. He leapt out of the car and opened my car door, tugging me out of the car. He shoved me over on the ground and grabbed my case out of the boot. He tossed it at me, then got back in the car and drove away.

I was sitting on the ground with my suitcase next to me. I burst into tears, managed to get up and pull my case further over to the side of the road. I didn't know what to do. I was done. I had lost everything. My phone was out of charge, and I had no strength. I was shattered. I must have sat there for at least thirty minutes when Fraser returned. He coolly pulled up next to me, wound down his window and, smirked. He ordered that I get back in the car. I collapsed into the passenger seat. I was numb. I couldn't think of a single word to say. Fraser put my case back in the car, and we drove away. Fraser said that we would go back to Danielle's and hope to God, that she would let us in. It was late when we arrived. Everybody was in bed, apart from Danielle. When she saw us on the doorstep, she told us that we looked dreadful. She invited us in and offered me a bath. It was heaven. Thank goodness for Danelle.

While I was in the bathroom I managed to connect to Facebook. I noticed a message from my good friend Carol. I hadn't seen her for a few years. We enjoyed our pregnancies at the same time. She wrote that her sister, Angelica lived about six hours from New York. Angelica had noticed on Facebook that I was living in The States. I quickly explained my situation. Carol seemed shocked. I was so thankful to hear back from Carol. She suggested that I try to get to a meeting point with Angelica. She could take me to her house. How on earth was I going to do that?

Carol took control, she advised me to persuade Fraser to meet Angelica in New Jersey. Somehow, I managed it. He agreed to take me the next day. I messaged Carol back to tell her that we would meet Angelica at 2:00 pm at a local diner in New Jersey. The next morning, I got up early to get ready to go. I didn't tell Danielle my plan, I didn't want to jinx it. Fraser took ages to get up, he was messing around on the phone all morning. Fraser seemed to be stalling. I kept telling him to get a move on; we were going to be late. We finally got in the car. Fraser put the keys in the ignition. The car wouldn't start. I noticed that he had been tinkering about with it during the morning. I thought that he was putting oil in it but apparently, he was on to me. I was frantic. I told him we needed to get there. I explained that Angelica had driven for over six hours to meet us. He said that this was a real shame, but that we weren't going. He strolled back into the house. I held my head in my hands and cried.

CHAPTER 15

Six Weeks to Turn it Around

I was goosed. My plan hadn't worked. I felt trapped. I went into the bathroom and connected straightaway on Facebook. I messaged Carol instantly to let her know what had happened. I apologised for wasting Angelica's time. Carol responded by saying that I 'shouldn't give that a second thought.' She explained that Angelica wanted to help me and told me not to worry. Carol assured me that we would come up with an alternate plan. I was crushed, I had missed my attempt to get away.

Carol had connected with my sister, Dina, on Facebook and informed her of my situation. Dina was really upset and worried. She had immediately contacted the British Embassy in London hoping that they could help to get me home. Dina was told that they couldn't help me because it 'appeared' like I was there by choice. Unless I was in actual danger, they were unable to get involved. At least three women knew my predicament. Even though I was devastated that my plan hadn't worked I also felt relieved that I had all of this support. Luckily, Fraser didn't know about it. At last, I had a lifeline. I went downstairs and sat at the kitchen table with Danielle and Fraser.

As I joined them at the table Fraser was sharing more plans. I was living in hope that I would be repaid, book my flight, and get the hell home. When Fraser went out to the back yard, I told Danielle that we had been sleeping in the car before we returned to her place. She told me that she didn't want me roughing it like that. She was embarrassed that Fraser would do that to me. I found myself for some strange reason being defensive and standing up for him again. I couldn't stop myself from being faithful to him.

When Fraser came back into the kitchen, he announced to Danielle that we were going to a meeting and that we would be back later. We drove across the Brooklyn Bridge to a neighbourhood bar. Fraser said that the bar hadn't been open long. When we went inside, I observed that it was quiet. It reminded me of the bar *'Cheers,'* in the US TV show. There were a couple of men sitting at the bar, drinking bottles of Budweiser, and munching away on the complimentary nuts. There was a pleasant fella behind the bar. Fraser ordered two coffees. Very soon, Fraser was engaged in conversation with the bartender, Greg, who turned out to be the owner. Gregg said that he had acquired the bar about six weeks ago, but that he was battling to attract customers. Red light, green light!

Fraser started inundating Greg with plans

for his bar. Here we go again, I thought. Fraser became increasingly excited, with Greg now hanging on his every idea. Fraser told him that we had moved into a large house in New Jersey, and that we "would be available to assist him." He explained that we were both retired but that we could turn his bar around 'standing on our heads.' He razzle dazzled Greg with karaoke possibilities, themed nights, curry nights, fun contests, and no end of promo opportunities. He even suggested that we could take his bar over for him. He told Greg, "Give us six weeks and we will turn this place around. It will be jumping in here." Then Fraser said, "We will be happy to do this for you for a small fee. We just need our expenses paid. No big deal." Greg was extremely, appreciative, delighted and proposed that we come back the next morning to discuss further plans. Fraser was puffed up like a peacock as we left the bar. As we got closer to the car, he practically danced a jig.

I found Brooklyn to be quite sinister. Fraser insisted that I never to go anywhere on my own. He said that being blonde and English would have me stick out like a sore thumb. He mentioned that there were parts of Brooklyn that were dangerous, that many people carried guns, and that they wouldn't think twice about using them. Fraser told me that I must stay with him, always. Obviously, he knew the area better than I did.

When we arrived at Danielle's house later that evening, she told us that she'd been bickering all afternoon with Lionel about us staying there. She told us that he wanted us both to leave, at once. Danielle apologised, though she explained that there was nothing she could do to change Lionel's mind. I felt sorry for her actually, as she was stuck in the middle. Lionel was right; we had stayed too long. This situation wasn't working out for any of us. We had to leave, tonight. Danielle discreetly sneaked $200 into my hand. She advised me to keep it from Fraser. Unfortunately, he noticed her giving me this money. We packed the car and left. I was sad to leave Danielle. We had become close. I genuinely liked her, as well as the kids. I now felt that I was exposed again and being alone with Fraser made me particularly uneasy. I had to be strong and clever.

We drove around aimlessly, once again. Eventually, we realized that we would have to sleep in the car. As usual, I couldn't sleep a wink. Fraser fell asleep almost instantly. Snoring and blowing his bad breath all over me. Revolting. I felt like running away.

I managed to check my texts while Fraser slept. I had received a text from Paul. He wrote that he had contacted Dina to ask if she'd heard from me. Paul was concerned about me, and Owen was missing me. Paul said that Owen was eager to talk to me. At last. I hoped that this was true. I was beginning to lose track of who was telling me the truth. Paul wanted me to call them both when I could. I deleted the text. I was so frightened.

When Fraser roused up, I told him that I needed to use the bathroom. It was about 5:00 am. We went to an all-night diner and I dashed to the bathrooms. I immediately called Paul. Thankfully, he picked up quickly. I was comforted to hear Paul's voice. I told him that I was in danger and that I was trapped in Brooklyn. He called me a 'stupid cow,' but he understood that this was serious. Paul said that he wanted to help me if he could. He assured me that he would call Dina as well as Carol. He said that they would all work together to make a plan to bring me back home. It was a massive relief for me to have some home contact, even if it was with Paul. I hurried back to the car. Fraser was ready to go. I was jumpy. What if he realised, I had been in contact with Paul? I felt like he knew. How would he? God knows but, by this time I was becoming paranoid.

When we arrived at the Brooklyn bar, Greg was sitting outside on a bar stool, having coffee. He asked us to sit with him. He offered us coffees, too. I wanted coffee more than he realized! Greg explained that his bar was a 'protected bar,' as were all the bars on that block. They were 'protected' by a man called, 'Big Jake.' This character was the head of the whole operation. Everyone feared him, including Greg. Fraser confirmed that he was well aware of 'Big Jake.' Greg believed that 'Big Jake' was due to visit the bar sometime soon to make a collection. Fraser seemed scared. His face drained of colour.

We all moved inside and went behind the bar. I took the opportunity to ask Fraser who this big shot, Jake was. He replied, fearfully, "Big Jake is someone you don't want to mess with. Greg is in serious danger if he doesn't pay Big Jake. He will break Greg's legs, 100% guaranteed!" I nervously giggled, saying, "That's ludicrous. This isn't the bloody Mafia, is it?" Fraser stared at me, stony faced, and said, "Oh yes, it is. This is the Mafia. If you see a big black car pull up outside, come and tell me and don't speak to anybody. When we are in this bar you mustn't go too far away from me. I promise that I will protect you."

A couple of weeks later, the bar was becoming more popular. Fraser was stealing from the till. Everything felt out of control. We managed to secure a few nights in cheap hotels. Fraser was becoming progressively more jealous. He wouldn't let me out of his sight and became angry with me if I chatted too long to any of the men. He was very calculating. I was becoming more afraid of him. He would frown at me from the other end of the bar. When I had my back turned to the bar, Fraser would whisper in my ear, telling me to stop flirting. He would make a point of informing anybody I chatted to that I was his wife. I turned into a nervous wreck. I tried to avoid conversations with anyone who may be sitting at the bar.

The first themed night we arranged was a James Bond theme. We placed flyers on car windshields nearby. As we drove around, I intentionally became acquainted with the area. Greg and his wife came to the James Bond Night. We were over the moon to see so many people join us; the bar was crowded. We had done it. Success!

At the end of the night, we were cashing up behind the bar. Suddenly, I heard a car screech to a halt outside the front door. It was a huge black limo, with the engine running. The driver opened the rear door. A large fella wearing glasses emerged from the car and sauntered into the bar. I told him that we were closed. He glowered at me. Fraser quietly whispered under his breath for me to "shut up." Fraser seemed terrified. He dashed to the front of the bar and went to shake the man's hand. Fraser quickly introduced himself, and then me, as his wife!

Greg had already heard the man's voice. He came scurrying out of the office and nodded at the man. They both went to the back yard. Fraser came back behind the bar. He was trembling. He informed me that this was none other than the infamous, 'Big Jake.' When I glanced outside, I noticed that the driver appeared to be searching the boot of the limo. Fraser scampered outside to offer him a drink. The driver slammed the car boot down and waved him off. Fraser sprinted back in. He warned me not to say a word. He told me that he had noticed a massive gun in the car. I didn't know whether to believe him.

A few minutes later, Greg appeared with Big Jake. They strolled out to the car, shook hands and Big Jake got into the back of the car, and they zoomed off. Greg was visibly shaking when he came back. He didn't say a word; he had poured himself a large whiskey. After quaffing his drink, Greg announced that, as the Bond night had been such a success, Big Jake demanded double the money every month. Greg was enraged, but there was nothing he could do. He had to pay up. It felt like I'd been an 'extra' in a bad movie. There was no doubt that these blokes were gangsters. They clearly meant every word they said. Greg warned us that we must make sure we delivered on our promises, or he would be waving goodbye to his bar, and his kneecaps.

We left for the night shortly after that. Fraser managed to steal sufficient money for a hotel, and a meal for us both. I was so tired I couldn't even care. Fraser was fast asleep by the time I got out of the bath and into bed. Thank God. I didn't want him near me, by then. His charm and charisma which had bewitched me at first, had worn very thin. Plus, his unpleasant breath was such a turn off. I avoided close contact with him as much as possible. I had lost count of how many times he had turned nasty or grabbed me by the throat. He was erratic and I couldn't run the risk of him getting out of control. We continued working at the bar everyday and I was living on hope that I would find a way out of this hellish situation very soon.

One lunchtime it was quiet in the bar. I was sitting at the bar on the laptop working on the music for the playlist. Fraser was in the back yard organising the tables. Suddenly, I felt the earth move and the bar shake. It was the most peculiar and scary feeling. I heard on the news later that there'd been an earthquake in NYC. So, that's what that was. I had heard about them in America but I never thought I would experience one. It certainly made me miss home. I was yearning to be back in England. I began to imagine how I would feel if I had been hurt in that earthquake and left to die so far away. I gazed up at the sky and tried to think of being back in Somerset. I began to cry. When I opened my eyes, I realized that I was still in this hell hole. This was another awakening. I just had to find my way back home.

Ever since I had contacted Paul, he had been sending me texts. He became my point of contact in the UK. Dina, Paul, and Carol had agreed that it was now time to let Mam know what was going on. She had been asking Dina if she had heard from me. Mam was beside herself when she heard about my situation. She desperately wanted to help to get me home. Paul told me that Mam offered to pay for a flight if I could get to the nearest airport. I hadn't a clue as to how I was going to achieve that. I couldn't get away from Fraser for longer than five minutes. I told Paul that I needed to strategize and that I'd get back to him as soon as I could. Paul told me to be careful but to hurry. He said that we needed to sort this out and get me back home. As if I didn't know that! Paul was always good at stating the obvious.

As it was always tricky to get a parking spot outside the bar, we often parked a couple of blocks away. I was frantically trying to work out a plan to get to an airport. One night, we didn't make sufficient money for a hotel. There were hardly any customers in the bar. I was shattered, my knees were swollen, and I felt despondent. More than any other night, I wanted a bed. It was dreadful. I couldn't face sleeping in the car again so I found the courage to speak up to Fraser. To my amazement, and relief, Fraser agreed and suggested that we find somewhere more comfortable to sleep. Oh joy! I was at my breaking point.

He brought me down the street to a derelict house. When he opened the door, it was beyond anything I had ever seen. It was absolutely horrendous. Staying there was another light bulb moment; perhaps the final one. I'd reached the point where I had had enough. I simply couldn't carry on like this. I felt that I would rather be dead. I was giving up hope. We had no home; there was no sign of my reimbursement and I finally accepted that it wasn't going to happen. What was important was that I find a way to get the hell away from Fraser. I needed to get home to my family. This man was a pathological liar. This was never going to end well.

This was it. I decided that, depending on where we parked the next day, I would run away. This was my chance. I had to go through with it, no doubt! I'd moved everything I needed into my smaller case. I made my mind up that if we parked a couple of blocks away from the bar, I would make an excuse to go back to the car. I planned to grab my small case and run. On the other hand, if we got a spot directly outside the bar, I wouldn't be able to do it. I was praying to all the Parking Gods in the world, that there wouldn't be a parking spot outside the bar.

When the sun came up that morning, I was certain that this was the day I would escape. I hauled myself up off the wooden floor and used the filthy bathroom. Luckily, I managed to get some running water but it was stone cold. I cleaned myself up as well as I could, peering through the cracks on the broken mirror above the sink. The time had come to leave. As we drove around to the bar, I was so fearful. I was holding my breath; waiting to find out where we would park. There were cars all the way up and down the road outside the bar. This was it. My moment.

Fraser groaned, as there were no spots left. I was overjoyed, but full of nerves. I was sure of my plan and I had to go through with it. My time with Fraser was up. I had to take this chance and break away. We parked about a block away from the bar. My mouth was dry and I was trembling. Fraser asked me if I was "okay" and told me that I looked terrible. I didn't say anything.

Usually, I took my iPad into the bar, so that I could use it to play music. I couldn't take it with me that day, because of my plan. I wondered how I would explain this to Fraser. I hadn't thought of that. Regardless, I managed to leave it in the car, without Fraser seeming to notice.

When we arrived at the bar, we went in and I went to my usual table. I grabbed Greg's laptop to prepare the music. Meanwhile, Fraser was messing around in the backyard. I mustered up the courage to tell him that I needed to pop back to the car. I said that I had left my medication, and my iPad. Typically, Fraser immediately offered to get them for me. He still didn't want me to be walking around on my own. I panicked but told him that it was better that I went, as I knew exactly where they were.

Fraser was extremely reluctant to let me go, at first. I insisted that I go and he hesitated but gave me the car keys. My hand was shaking as I took them. Despite his behaviour, a small part of me felt sad that this hadn't worked out. As I left, he hollered, "Hurry back. There are some dodgy people around this place." By this time, I was certain that Fraser was one of the dodgiest people!

    Shaking from top to toe, I hoped and prayed that Fraser wouldn't follow me, though I was confident he couldn't leave the bar. Greg wasn't there yet. I turned and took one last look at him, as I walked towards the door. At this point, I felt that I never wanted to see his face, or hear his voice, again. I was finished. Slowly but surely, he had attempted to destroy my spirit. As I left the bar, my legs became weak and my hands were clammy. I was panic stricken. I don't remember ever being that scared. Goodness knows how, but I found the strength to run around the corner. I was sweating. When I reached the car, it seemed to take me ages to unlock it. My hands were shaking so much that I couldn't keep them still enough to put the key in the door. I kept nervously looking behind me, praying that Fraser hadn't followed me.

    I popped open the boot of the car and grabbed my case. Then, I ran to the passenger door, yanked it open, grabbed my iPad, and ripped open the glove box. I was horrified to discover a gun! I froze, then I pulled myself together. Oh my god, was I ever doing the right thing! I threw the keys in the glove box, slammed it shut and slammed the front door, as well. I grabbed my case and ran as fast as I could. I was so choked. I could barely breathe. I felt like I couldn't get any air.

I was aware that there was a police station a couple of blocks away. I had noticed it when we had been leaflet dropping. I was praying that I was heading in the right direction. My whole body turned to jelly. As I approached the Police Station, I started to cry. I nearly tripped over my feet as I was nervously looking behind me. I was petrified that Fraser was going to see me. I even thought that I would wind up running past the bar, and he'd chase me. I was sweating and felt sick. I kept running and tugging my case as fast as I could. I felt on the brink of collapse. As I ran around the next corner, I saw police cars parked outside the police station. The relief was immense. I hurried across the road, as fast as I could, dodging cars. Finally, I burst through the station doors. I collapsed on the floor, dropping my case on the way.

A female officer was sitting behind the screen. Several others were milling around. They all stopped and looked at me. The female officer came towards me from behind the screen. I was sprawled on the floor, crying hysterically. I couldn't speak. I could hardly draw a breath.

I had done it. I had escaped. I couldn't stop trembling. The police officer brought me a blanket and a chair. She suggested that I try to calm down. She asked me what was wrong. It felt like ages until I could speak. My teeth were chattering together, uncontrollably. My mouth wouldn't seem to work! Eventually, I told her that I was from England. I explained that I had been conned by a man via Facebook. I kept telling her that he was dangerous and that he was in a bar around the corner. I believed that I was in real danger. I pleaded with her to go and arrest Fraser. I told her about the whole thing in the space of around a minute. Once I started, I couldn't stop talking. I told her that I'd been foolish and that I was ashamed. I felt embarrassed. I was rambling and couldn't get my words out fast enough. I repeated that I had been conned and that I was penniless.

    The officer took hold of my shoulders, shook me slightly and said, "Honey, you have done a very brave thing. You are no longer in danger. If you had stayed with him, you would have been leaving here in a body bag, guaranteed." She told me that there are so many women scammed, but don't escape the situation. She said that I should consider myself very brave and by no means foolish.

    After a cup of tea, I quietened down. I told the officer that my mother could arrange a flight home for me. She asked me if I knew anyone other than Fraser in NYC. I replied that I knew Fraser's sister, Danielle. She suggested that she should call Danielle. I panicked and said that I didn't want to go back to her place. I was scared in case Fraser turned up. I didn't want to run the risk. The officer told me that I couldn't stay at the police station. I pleaded with her to arrest Fraser. I told her that he had assaulted me several times. I said that he was a pathological liar, and a dangerous man. She didn't seem to be interested in that. She was more concerned about getting me back to England.

Eventually, she offered to drive around to the bar. I told her that I had another suitcase in the car a couple of blocks away. She suggested that we drive around to grab my suitcase. Then, I could show her where to find Fraser. When we got to where the car was parked, it had gone. We drove to the bar, but it was closed. Fraser had got away. We drove back to the police station and called Danielle. I explained to her that I had run away from Fraser. I told her the whole story within seconds, including that we had been sleeping rough, again. I said that I was finished. We both cried. Danielle reassured me and told me not to worry. She promised me that she would come straightaway. She agreed that she would help me book the flight home. The police confirmed that they would place a patrol car outside Danielle's house. This would make certain that Fraser wouldn't come to the house. I tried everything to get them to arrest Fraser. I told them that he had broken his child support agreement in Tennessee. Eventually, the police assured me that they would check him out. Somehow, I didn't believe them.

When we arrived at Danielle's, she admitted that Fraser had been constantly swearing at her down the phone. She said that he told her that I had left him, that he was crying one minute, then the next he was vile, and furious. He threatened that he would kill me if he found me. Danielle repeatedly told him that she hadn't heard from me. She said that she didn't have any idea where I might be. She told him that even if she did know where I was, she wouldn't tell him, anyway. Fraser was furious and threatened to burn her house down. Danielle told him that he was a sick man and a liar. He certainly was.

After we talked, Danielle rang Mam. As soon as I heard her voice, I cried. I asked Danielle to explain the situation for me. We found a flight for the following day, from Newark direct to Gatwick. Mam confirmed that she would ask Dina to book the flight but she would pay for it. I was going home. Thank God. My ordeal was over.

After a stressful night, Danielle took me to the airport, with her girls. I was so appreciative to her for helping me. I was sad to be leaving them. I had grown fond of them. I said my 'goodbyes' and walked to Departures. I simply couldn't wait to get on the flight.

Anxiously, I checked in and went through to 'Departures.' I was worried in case there was a problem with my passport. I had clearly gone over my holiday visa dates. I was on edge, watching everyone, and expecting to see Fraser at any moment. My mobile rang, just as I was going through to 'Departures.' I picked it up. It was Fraser. Sheer terror. Fraser told me that he was at the airport and that he wanted to say 'goodbye.' I quickly told him that I couldn't wait. He pleaded with me to meet him at the 'Departures' gate so that he could see me off. He told me that he understood that I had to leave. But that he wanted to say 'goodbye.' Even though I was shaking, sweating, panicking and terrorised, I somehow found the strength to tell him that I wasn't going to wait. My flight was boarding. Fraser begged me to wait, saying that he was in the car park. I wavered for a few seconds. Why? I was so traumatised; I hadn't a clue what I was feeling. I suddenly pulled myself together as the last call came. I realized that I couldn't wait any longer. I got through the gates. I boarded the plane to Gatwick.

PART THREE

PICKING UP THE PIECES

CHAPTER 16

Sweet Tea & Seagulls - 2011

I never felt such massive relief to be on English soil in my life. I don't believe I ever will again. There were many times during those eight months when I wasn't sure if I would ever return to my homeland. When the wheels finally touched down at Gatwick Airport I just burst into tears. Finally, I felt relief and gratitude. I was safe. Thank God I was home, at last.

    I grabbed my bag and got off the plane. It was chilly and I didn't have a coat because all my clothes were left in America. I was trembling with the cold, as well as the trauma of my great escape. Thankfully, I breezed through customs with no problems. I had one last step, however. I was worried that I wouldn't be allowed back into the country as I was so far over my visa dates. I couldn't contemplate being sent back. I stumbled towards Arrivals and urgently looked for Paul. This was so different from the day I flew out to Nashville. I was so different. That day, I was vibrant, sparkly, and healthy, bouncing through the airport with excitement about my future. I was filled with hope and optimism. Now, I didn't know if I would ever trust anyone again; as I felt that I had made such an almighty mistake. I had often read magazine articles about women being conned and was quite judgemental about them. I never dreamed that this could happen to me.

I didn't see Paul but I heard him. He was describing his version of my story to one of the security blokes. I walked around the corner and there he was. When he noticed me, he immediately marched over, holding his arms open wide. I let him wrap me up in them. When we got into the car I fell into a daze as Paul drove. As he banged on with a wall of words, I was having flashbacks of the US and of Fraser. I was replaying the journey backwards. I was nowhere near unravelling the physical and emotional effects I had experienced. I didn't know if I would ever be able to. Also, as we drove along, the love for the English countryside was so soothing. The silver birch and the sweet chestnut trees, the ivy covered farm fences, and the cows in the fields; I was in love with it all. I also had a feeling of safety. With Fraser from one minute to the next there was none of that. I had no idea how much my nervous system had been attacked and how much I needed the routine and certainty of my Somerset life. Possibly, I could heal.

Dina had suggested that I must go straight to Hackness to stay with her, but Paul knew that I wanted to see Owen first so we went there. I asked Paul to share with me every little thing about Owen that I had missed in the past eight months. Paul responded dismissively by just telling me that Owen was okay and that he would be delighted to have me back. It was extremely late when we arrived at the house. Paul offered me the bedroom and that he would sleep on the sofa, thankfully. I had absolutely no intention of going back with him.

I woke up early the next morning to the sound of the door closing as Paul went off to work. I had become a light sleeper. I got up and took a blanket out to sit in the garden. It was so good to hear the seagulls. They used to annoy the hell out of me back in the day. Now they were music to my ears. I closed my eyes, put my head back and listened to the seagulls and all the other birds. I recalled the many times being outside on the patio of the bar in Brooklyn when I had looked up to the sky and dreamt that I was back in Somerset; and now I finally was. Our cat Cosmo came sauntering over to me and jumped up on my lap. We were so pleased to see each other. I had almost forgotten about Cosmo. I tickled his belly.

Owen came out to join me in the garden. I jumped up, dropped the blanket, and ran to him. I held on to him for dear life. I couldn't speak. I sobbed and sobbed; so did Owen. We held on to each other for ages. I didn't want to let him go, ever again. I felt my heart physically aching as I held Owen close to me. I realised how much I had missed him and how much I love him. Eventually, we let go of each other and Owen pulled up a chair to sit next to me. We sat in silence for a while, taking the moment in. I didn't know how to begin talking to him. I had so much that I wanted to say and so much that I was afraid to say. I wanted to ask him why he had decided to go back to his dad, and why he wouldn't speak to me at that time. Even so, I remained silent. I couldn't believe that I had finally found my way back to him. I genuinely thought that I would never see him, or any of my family, again. The relief was tremendous. We sat together listening to the birds, enjoying the peace, and tickling the Cosmo's belly. I could have sat there forever. Owen didn't seem to know where to begin, either. Suddenly, he asked me the million-dollar question, "Why did you go to America, Mum?"

That question! Owen had every right to ask this of me. I took a huge breath before I could reply. At this point in my process of unravelling I felt that there was nothing I could say to justify such a crazy decision to go to America, especially alone. I wanted to find something honest to say to my son. I had to dig deeper to find my truth. I genuinely believed that Fraser was somebody I could trust. Fraser and I had spoken for over five months about exciting business opportunities for me. I felt that we were good friends.

I explained to Owen that when I first arrived,

I had absolutely every intention of staying for only ten days. I was utterly convinced that there was a business opportunity that would benefit our whole family, with my new friend. I was certain that I would be hired by Fraser to run his offices in London. I told Owen that even though I had a return ticket for ten days after my American arrival, my passport went missing the day before I was due to fly home. I later found out that Fraser had it. I stopped there. I couldn't speak anymore. I started to cry. It was so difficult to admit that and so much more to Owen. I was nowhere near ready. We decided to talk more later in the day.

The wall of words continued with Paul. He didn't seem to have any empathy. He simply didn't understand. He kept staring at me in disbelief and continued pushing me for answers I wasn't ready to give. I was slowly becoming aware of the quagmire of emotions I was swimming in. I knew it was going to be a long process of healing. Paul had no capacity to help me at this time. I was traumatised and would have to move to clarity in my own way and in my own time.

It was beginning to be time for me to work out what I was going to do next. Where to go from here? It was clear to me that my future was not with Paul. This much I knew.

I chose to stay quiet. I needed to rebuild my mental strength. I felt that I needed to come to terms with parts of myself. How did I allow this and why would I allow this? What actually woke me up? What had I learned from this? I couldn't explain these things to myself, yet. I knew that I had to unravel and process this; hopefully sooner than later. I still needed time to reacclimate to 'normal life.' Honestly, I still couldn't string a sentence together. I needed this quiet in the garden with my sweet English cup of tea. The smallest things that I had taken for granted before were now such gifts. When I had so very little, that's when I realised that possessions didn't matter. People did. Relationships did. How we live together with our heart is what matters. While in my quiet, I was also desperately trying to make sense of my time in America. I had constant flashbacks to Nashville, Belmont Park, and the Brooklyn Bar. It was all surreal, and I still couldn't comprehend what I had actually been through and why.

    A few days later, Paul and Owen were busy tinkering with the Mazda in the garage when my mobile rang. When I answered it, to my horror, it was Fraser. I shuddered. My blood ran cold. Suddenly, the phone felt boiling hot. I pressed 'End' and threw it on the floor. A few minutes later it rang again. I was afraid that he was in England, so I answered. I wanted an explanation from him. I was also curious to hear what lies were going to come out of his stinking mouth. Before I could speak, Fraser begged,

"Don't put the phone down, Baby." I cringed. Don't call me baby.

Fraser tearfully told me that he was sorry. He began telling me that everything he had told me was the truth. He begged me to believe him. He said that he loved me and that he would never lie to me. He said that everyone else was lying, not him. He claimed that they were all nuts. I impatiently listened to his ceaseless rambling when I interrupted him and told him that I was never coming back. I was home. I told him that he owed me over £20,000 and that I wanted it back, every single penny. He shot back saying that I would only get my money back, when I returned to the States, but not before. What planet was he on? How stupid did he think I was? His arrogance was astonishing. If he wasn't so pathetic and I wasn't so angry, I would find him laughable. Was I being pranked? Where was the camera? From my perspective standing in my kitchen, I could see that this was all so ludicrous.

Fraser continued his tirade and then pathetically he told me that he had been ill and that maybe he had cancer. Oh Jesus! How low would this man go to get me back? He must have been so desperate, to use that line. I just told him that unless he was giving me the details of my £20,000 money transfer, I didn't want to hear anything else. Then his true feelings came out. He rudely called me a 'dumb English fuck,' and told me to 'Go fuck myself,' and hung up. An expensive lesson to be sure and I learned it. Onward and upward for me now.

Now I felt strong enough to see my family. So first I arranged to meet Sarah for a coffee. I was so excited to see her. I was desperate to make sure she was ok and I was nervous too. I didn't really know what she thought of my American adventure. When she walked into the cafe, she was bursting with confidence. She looked amazing, and incredibly happy. In true Sarah style, she looked me straight in the eyes and asked, "Well, what the fuck was that all about, then?" Trust Sarah to break the ice. We both fell about laughing. I could count on Sarah to get straight to the point and to make the situation funny. Sarah was happy with her new job. She was enjoying sharing a flat with her friend and having a blast. What a delight it was to have mother and daughter banter. Again, appreciating the things I took for granted before.

CHAPTER 17

Full Circle

Ok, next on the list. It was time to deal with Paul and the divorce. I had swiftly thrown the dress ring from Fraser in the rubbish bin at the airport. I didn't need any needless questions about my being 'engaged' to the American bloke from Paul. I definitely wanted to go ahead with the divorce, whether Paul liked it or not. I decided to keep it to myself for the moment to keep the lid on Paul.

I made an appointment to see my solicitor while Paul was at work. At this point, I didn't want Paul to freak out about it. My solicitor already knew about my trip out of the country. She informed me that Paul had turned up while I was away without an appointment. As usual, Paul enjoyed embellishing stories about me. His newest one was that I had lost my mind and 'disappeared' to America. With his typical arrogance, he instructed her to close my file, as he thought that I wouldn't be coming back. Of course, she told him that she couldn't do that, as Paul wasn't her client and she couldn't discuss anything with him. I confirmed that I definitely wanted my divorce to go ahead. I was worried that I couldn't pay her expensive fees. She told me not to worry as she would deduct her fees from any settlement. She encouraged me to push for a financial settlement.

To be fair to Paul, I decided to let him know that night that I had instructed my solicitor to go ahead with the divorce. I realized that this was going to be a challenging and upsetting conversation, but it had to be done. I felt that I couldn't keep putting it off. Paul was racing ahead and making future plans for us. I didn't need things to escalate. Paul was unrelenting; he never stopped banging on about our future together. He was making plans for all sorts of ventures for us. As I knew I wasn't going to be part of any of these plans and I wasn't going to be staying, I had to be honest with him. I didn't want to lead him on.

When I returned, Owen was in the garden. I went outside to join him, and Cosmo. This was quickly becoming our favourite place and a regular thing for us; something we both enjoyed. As I sat next to him, he said that he knew that his dad and I were never going to work. He believed that we were too different and incompatible. He saw Paul driving me mad. I was impressed, not to mention proud, of how grown up and wise my son had become. He added, "I think you should go North to Gran and Aunty Dina. With Dad, I've noticed that you're really tense and anxious. I want you to be happy, Mum, and I don't think you can be here." Owen was an awesome and clever boy for his age. Thank goodness that Owen could see the truth and help me see it, as well.

I was so relieved that he could see the bigger picture and was so supportive. So, I asked Owen, "Why don't you come with me?" He answered, "No, Mum, I think its best that you go on your own. I'll be fine with Dad here. I feel that it's time for you to put yourself first. You need to make a fresh start. Once you get settled there, I'll come and stay with you for a bit." I felt so sad at the prospect of leaving Owen as I had only just got back. He sensed this and added, "You know, you can always come down here to see Sarah and me, any time. You can stay with your friend, Janie." We both cried and hugged. I knew that he was right. I couldn't believe how understanding he was. There was only one problem. How was I going to break the news to Paul? I didn't want him to lose it. Owen and I agreed that I needed to 'pick my moment.' That opportunity seemed far away.

Paul must have sensed that something was amiss. Instead of trying to talk to me, he started to get frustrated with me. He came home from work one day and told me that I needed to get back in the 'real world.' This was my chance. I told Paul that I agreed and that it was time for me to see my family. He seemed quite relaxed for once. I let him know that his future plans were not going to include me. He became tearful. I hadn't seen him like that for ages. The penny was dropping. I talked about our relationship and how different we were from each other. I explained that I was hugely grateful to him for all of his help, especially getting me back from America. He started to sob his heart out. It was heartbreaking to see him like that. He kept saying that he'd married me for life and that I was the love of his life. He said that he didn't think for a minute when we got married, that we would ever get divorced. He confirmed that he genuinely loved me.

I felt dreadful but I knew that this was best for us both. I finally realised how strong I was. Even though I hated watching him being so broken, I felt compassion for him. I truly hoped that I had not misled him. I knew that deep down we never should have married in the first place. I got swept away with it all. When we met at that time, he was the right person for me. He was strong and honestly my knight in shining armour. Over time as life would have it, we grew apart. To be fair to Paul, I wasn't what he needed either, we were like oil and water.

When Paul calmed down. I told him that I did love him for the place that he held in my life. I cared about him and wanted the best for him. He countered that he expected me to fall back in love with him; if only I would give him the chance. I explained that this was never going to happen. It was never my intention to break his heart, either.

Paul was uncharacteristically quiet for the next few days. We had very little conversation. A day later over coffee, Paul mentioned that he'd been thinking and handed me a bus ticket to Hackness. He seemed to have accepted that I wanted to see my family. It was a return ticket for a week. I thanked him and mentioned that Owen had suggested that it would be a good idea for me to stay up North for a bit longer. Paul's face dropped with shock and he told me that I was lying, as 'Owen would never suggest such a thing.' He became instantly angry. Owen was in his bedroom. He heard our conversation and came right out into the lounge. Owen asked Paul to calm down and confirmed that he thought I should stay with my family. He thought I'd be better off with them, for a while. Paul became even more agitated, as it finally dawned on him that I was leaving for good. I could see the panic in his face as he yelled, "You planned it all. You never wanted to stay with me!" I replied, "I've been trying to tell you that I was leaving, I didn't want to hurt you. I thought that I made this clear in our conversations." He was stomping around the house and punching the walls. He hollered, "You used me! You're so ungrateful after all I've done for you! You bitch!" I tried to reason with him, remind him of our conversations, and encourage him to calm down. There was clearly no hope of that; he was on a roll. I was frightened, as he seemed to be losing control. I could see his face changing from love to pure hate. He was turning. I started trembling.

    I tried repeatedly to reason with him, but he wouldn't listen to me. He was losing it more and more. He screamed, "Get out. Now!" I panicked. Owen looked terrified. He asked Paul to calm down again. He wouldn't listen to him, either. Paul hurried into the kitchen, opened the drawer, and snatched a huge carving knife, which he lunged at me. I froze completely. I didn't know what to do. Owen immediately rang the police. I heard Owen explaining that his dad had 'lost the plot.' He said that he was waving a knife around at his mother. I ran into the bedroom and slammed the door. Paul followed and stood outside the door screaming when the police arrived. Owen opened the front door and let two female officers into the house.

    As soon as Paul saw them, before the police could see him, he dropped the knife. He told them that I was the 'nutter' and that I had triggered a row. They asked him why Owen had reported that he was waving a knife around. Paul told them that it had been me who was brandishing the knife. I cautiously opened the bedroom door and stepped into the hallway. I was desperately hoping that Owen would tell them the truth, but he kept silent. He seemed afraid. The police insisted that Paul move away from me. They said that they needed to talk to me in private. The officers and I went back into the bedroom. They asked me what was going on. I told them my version of the events. Paul kept shouting through the door and saying that I was a liar and that I was 'off my head.' He also said that I had lost my mind and gone to America with a stranger I had met online. He told them that this was his house and that he wanted me out. I was trembling. I didn't know what was going to happen next. I was hoping that Paul would back down. What on earth was I going to do? I tried to catch Owen's attention, but he had disappeared into the lounge so I couldn't see him.

It was about 7:00 pm and the officers informed me that I had to leave. They said that because this was Paul's house, I was the one who should leave. I pleaded with them and clarified that this was my home too. Paul was silent, standing behind them staring at me. They asked me if there was anyone I could ring. I rang Sarah but she was camping with a friend so she couldn't help me. She told me to get out of the house, and away from Paul. I told the police that I had a bus ticket to Hackness but that it wasn't valid until the following day.

The officers gave me no choice. They said that I had to go with them, right then. They offered to take me to the bus station and that I would need to wait for the coach. I didn't think that I would be able to get on a coach that night. They didn't seem to care. They said that it wasn't their problem. They flatly refused to let me remain at 'Paul's house.' Not acknowledging that it had been my home too.

By this time, Paul and Owen were in the lounge. Owen was extremely upset, though he didn't say anything. I took the officers up on their offer so I left with them. I didn't even get a chance to say goodbye to my son. I grabbed my handbag and a carrier bag with some toiletries, my phone charger, mobile and sank into the back of the Police car. As we drove out of the cul-de-sac, Owen was standing in the doorway, looking in my direction at a loss. I understood his loyalty to both his dad and me. This was certainly not the way I wanted my marriage with Paul to end.

I didn't say a word on the way to the coach station. The police officers turfed me out of the patrol car and mentioned that there was a bus due around midnight. I had three hours to wait. I tried the door to the waiting room but it was locked, so I sat down on the bench outside the waiting room. There were people I could call but I was embarrassed and I wanted to do this on my own. So, I chose to just wait, and hope to God that the driver of the coach was sympathetic and would let me get on the blessed coach.

While I was waiting, I rang Carol and told her what had happened. I was distraught. Carol was as calm as ever. She told me not to worry, that she would pick me up whatever time I arrived and that I could stay with her. She suggested that I keep my phone charged and let her know which coach I caught. I managed to calm down, for the moment.

Just before midnight, the coach pulled into the station. It was half empty. I climbed the couple of steps and looked at the driver. I burst into tears. He asked me what was wrong. I told him that I had a ticket, but it was for the morning coach. He waved his arm and told me to 'jump on.' I collapsed onto my seat and breathed a huge sigh of relief. I rang Owen. I wanted to reassure him that I understood why he had called the police. He must have been terrified seeing his dad wielding a knife at his Mum. I also wanted to let him know that I had got on the coach and was safely on my way to London.

I was in a daze all the way to London. I must have slept on and off. It was about 5:00 am when we arrived at Victoria Station. I tripped off the coach and gazed up at the departures board and noticed that my next coach to Hackness was at 11:00 am. I sat on a bench at the coach stand. At last, my coach came in, and I climbed aboard.

Eventually, we arrived at Hackness. As we drove through the town, I wondered what was to become of me. It felt good to be home. I stared out of the window and caught a glimpse of Carol standing at the coach stand. I got off the coach and cried instantly, again. Carol had tears in her eyes, as well. She gave me a massive hug and assured me that I was going to be okay. She promised me that she would look after me. I was back where I belong.

CHAPTER 18

Genuine Solid People – 2011/12

As we drove to Carol's house I was inundated with flashbacks. A million things were going through my head, all at once. The image of Brutus still haunted me. I remembered meeting Donovan at the Dentist, giving birth to my cherished children, Tyler, Sarah, and Owen. It felt like I was watching a movie about my life, and everything that I had gone through.

When we got to Carol's lovely home, she made us a cup of tea. It all felt surreal, being back in Hackness, where everything had begun. I couldn't think clearly and felt very much alone although, Carol had such a calming effect on me. She just exuded care and love. I hadn't a clue what I was going to do next. Carol suggested that I must take things slowly, take a deep breath and get myself together first. She was so comforting and reassuring; allowing me to feel that everything was going to be okay. She said that I was a strong survivor. She told me that I was safe with her. Every nicety she said made me cry again. What the hell had happened to me? Nothing made any sense to me.

Carol lived with her husband, Ethan and her youngest son, Bobbie. As they were all out working, she gave me a key to come and go as I please. She told me to treat her place like my home. Carol and I talked for hours. I was feeling so bewildered about everything. I didn't know how to start untangling it all. Carol was incredibly patient, even though she had exhausting days at work. She would listen to me; never judging me. She knew me very well. She told me that she had sensed what was going on with Donovan. She remembered her visits to the house and witnessed how demanding he was. She recalled the times when he criticised the sandwich I had made for him or that the tea was too hot. She knew my heartbreak when I needed to leave Tyler and Sarah with him.

Bit by bit, step by step I started moving on and becoming independent. I applied for an emergency payment from the DSS. To my surprise I got £200, which I would need to pay back when I got a job. Carol took me into Hackness early one morning because I needed to open a bank account. After that, we went shopping at 'preloved' shops where I bought some fun work and weekend clothes. I had almost run out of makeup, too, so I replenished my stock. I had missed my lippy. I was slowly coming back to life, piece by piece, and it felt good.

Mam lived near Carol, so she took me to see her the day after I arrived. When I came into the house it was like I had never been away from

Mam. She was sort of teary but held it all in so I did, as well. I went to see her every day after that. We would talk for hours while she watched the Channel 4 Horse Racing. We chatted about her life, and sometimes we would browse through her photo albums. There were so many things that I discovered that I didn't know about her childhood, and teenage years. I realised how little I knew of Mam's earlier life. So, I asked her loads of questions and got surprising answers that were funny, touching, and meaningful. So much I didn't know. I was so grateful that I had this time with her and something more. Something opened up in me; a space in me. I felt that I had room for Mam. I really wanted to know her life. I wanted to understand her from this present place in my life. I really cared. I loved talking to her, and she made me laugh. Mam had a wicked sense of humour, and mine was starting to come back slowly through our talks. Mam was incredibly careful and she didn't press me to answer questions about America, or Paul. We would talk about Tyler, Sarah, and Owen though. She was immensely proud of Tyler with the band and wanted to know all about that. I informed her of his performance schedule and that they were recording an album. She was thrilled for Tyler, as he had been through so much with his health. It was so exciting and beyond impressive.

    My dear friends Amy and Mike lived close

to Carol. Years ago, we went our separate ways. I felt that they weren't comfortable with Donovan's behaviour. I wasn't sure how I would be received. I wanted to see Amy and contemplated it for a few days. Eventually, I found the courage to knock on her door. She came to the glass doors, and when she saw me standing there, her face beamed. I had missed that great big smile. She was surprised to see me and burst out of the door to wrap her arms around me. She had heard that I was living in America. She said that she thought she would never see me again. I was over the moon to see her, and relieved that she was clearly pleased to see me. She had so many questions for me, all at a hundred miles an hour. I was speechless to start with. Where the hell do I start? I hadn't seen her for years, so I had so much to tell her and I wanted to hear about her life too. We had so much to catch up on. We must have sat together for hours while she listened intently to my story. We both kept crying. She couldn't believe what I had been through. Actually, when I was telling her, I couldn't believe it myself. I felt as if I was talking about someone else, not me. How could this by my story? Amy kept repeating, "Bloody, hell! You couldn't make this up! You should write a book!" I laughed it off, of course.

Mike bounced in from work. He had been pricing jobs for his roofing business. He was delighted to see me and gave me a massive hug. He asked me where the hell had I been. I felt like I had only seen them both yesterday and that I had never been away. I felt so welcome and comfortable. Amy told him that she would fill him in later, but that he wouldn't believe it. Mike asked me if I had seen their 'pub.' I was puzzled. I hadn't a clue what he was talking about. He reminded me about the time Paul and I had been visiting Sarah and Tyler and we popped in to see them. There was a huge shed in the garden on the right of the grass lawn. Mike told us that one day this would be his 'pub.' I remember that we all laughed at him, pulling his leg about it at the time. He just insisted that it was definitely going to happen.

Mike took me into his shed. I was shocked to see his old shed turned into a 'pub' with memorabilia strewn everywhere. He had collected stuff from auctions and eBay. There was a large picture of Elvis on the wall and tankards all over the ceiling. There was even an upright piano in the corner of the 'room.' It was amazing. What a fun space and such an achievement. The bar was in the corner with optics. There was a 'wall of fame' from all of their parties, too. This was a happy place, a party place. I was really excited to see it and could imagine the fun memories we would make. Little did I know how right I would be. We sat at the bar all afternoon and into the evening enjoying nibbles and sips. I was really happy to enjoy them. What a laugh we had. It was such fun. I had friends. Real friends. Genuine solid people who cared about me and I cared about them. I was home. I knew then that this was where I was meant to be.

We talked about the old times when I was living with Jackie and all of our ridiculous antics. Such fond memories. Amy called Jackie to tell her I was back. Jackie was ecstatic to hear that and said that she would arrange to see me soon. Jackie was now married with two children. I couldn't wait to see her. When I left the 'pub,' I had a massive smile on my face. I had found my sense of fun and humour again. It was a good feeling, I knew I was 'coming back' to life, again.

It was Christmastime and Carol always attended the Christingle church service on Christmas Eve, so I went with her. She told me that someone else usually went with her. She wouldn't tell me who as she wanted to surprise me. When we arrived, I was delighted to see Little Eileen at the door. Amy was there, too. It was so good to see Little Eileen. I had been thinking about seeing her, though I was nervous about it. I hadn't seen her for years. We had lost touch. It turned out that Carol and Little Eileen worked together and they had met a few years ago.

The Christingle service was magical. The place fell into darkness. Slowly all the candles from the back of the church began to light up the room. Strange and dramatic maybe, though I felt like every candle was a sign that my life was coming together. This was my chance. A fresh start. I wasn't going to mess it up this time. I felt quite proud of myself. I had hope. I looked up to the high ceiling and thanked God as well as all my 'angels' for getting me home.

Christmas was a tough time for me usually as I wasn't able to spend it with Sarah and Owen. I missed them so much. Tyler was usually away with the band. I spent this Christmas morning with Carol, then called in to see Mam on the way to spend the rest of the day with Amy and Mike. What a laugh we had. Singing songs and dancing around enjoying more nibbles and sips. I hadn't felt this happy for ages. I was getting stronger every day. Carol encouraged me to start running again. What a great idea. I ran and ran. I loved it. I felt free when I ran. Every step I took helped me heal and restored my spirit.

It was a New Year, so I decided it was time to look for work. I registered with an agency and within a couple of weeks I had landed a job at a small firm of solicitors in Hackness. I felt like I had won the lottery when I got my first month's salary. As I was staying with Carol, I insisted on paying rent. That felt good. I used to pop in on Mam after work most days and spent a lot of time with her at the weekends.

After a few weeks, Amy and Mike told me

that they had another house in Hackness. It was a one bedroom terrace house. The current tenant was leaving. They said that I was very welcome to rent it if I wanted to and that they would reduce the rent. Money was going to be tight, though I knew I could afford it. I looked at the house and thought that it was ideal. Carol had been so generous in allowing me to stay with her for the last three months. I felt it was time for me to move on though.

Amy and Mike furnished the house for me. They did an amazing job and I literally just had to walk in and put the kettle on. I must admit, it was really strange being on my own. I missed Carol and our talks. I started to wonder if I had rushed into moving out, though it was too late. I had done it. Everyone was busy with their own lives so I needed to start rebuilding mine.

I had been to see Dina a few times since I came back. She was incredibly happy that I was back in the North. She was busy working at a university in Leathley so I didn't see much of her during the week. She occasionally came to Mam's on Sundays, along with Harry. I caught up with them then.

I reconnected with Evangeline and she invited me over for the weekend. It was great to see her. We talked for hours while we sat in her lovely garden. She had moved to a bigger place and had a magical garden. It was peaceful with fairy lights, lanterns and the sound of windpipes hanging in her trees. I told her that I was keen to get to Somerset to see Sarah and Owen. She told me that Paul had been in touch with her. He had been trying to persuade her to leave Ged and move in with him! She was flabbergasted, as was I. What the hell? What was this even about? She thought that he was a desperate man and creepy.

Yet another step forward. I was thinking of getting a car. Evangeline and I were chatting away when she told me that her friend had a Renault that I could have. It was in her driveway, and she had lost her license so she couldn't drive it. We went to look at it straightaway. I took it like a shot. A free car? No brainer! Evangeline taxed it for me and wouldn't take a penny for that. How fortunate am I to have amazing friends? I was really delighted to have some wheels. I arranged to pick it up the following weekend. I loved it. It felt good having my independence again. I whizzed around in it and popped here, there, and everywhere. I bought some eyelashes for the front lights. It was my fun car. Everyone laughed as I drove past them and pointed at the great big diamante eyelashes. It was fun.

Little Eileen and I went off to the coast for a girl's weekend. It was so fun. That was my first 'long' journey in the Renault, and it went well. From then on, I had no worries about going long distances. We stayed at a grand hotel near the seafront and went out for an Italian dinner. It was such fun listening to songs by Whitney Houston on the journey over there. We talked about my leaving Donovan, which I felt had always been a bit of an elephant in the room with her. I was never really sure what she thought about the whole situation. I felt that she may have judged me for leaving Tyler and Sarah all those years ago. I couldn't have been more wrong. She explained that she didn't want to get involved at the time, but that she knew exactly what Donovan was like. She knew he was a devoted and patient father; but a nightmare to me. She said that she didn't blame me at all. What a relief! This had been bothering me for years. I didn't want her to think badly of me; as she was such a treasured friend.

I decided that I would take a long weekend off work and go on another trip to see my kids. So, off I went to Somerset. I was anxious driving that far on my own and wasn't certain of the way. It took me hours. A few days before I had asked my dear friend and neighbour Janie in Somerset if her offer still stood for me to stay with her. Without hesitation, she said that she would be delighted to have me. I felt so relieved as she felt like 'home.' Being mums of little ones together was so bonding all those years ago. Those relationships are just so special, she was my first and longest friend in Somerset to this day.

It was heavily raining most of the way. I could

hardly see the road in front of me. I was praying that my car wouldn't let me down. I must have held my breath for about thirty miles! I arrived at Janie's quite late. Once again, somebody who loved me put the kettle on, and we talked until the early hours. I told her of my painful American adventure. She couldn't quite believe what I had been through. She and so many were saying, "You wouldn't even want to make this up." She told me that Paul's version of events was much different to mine; oh, what a surprise! She was astounded when I told her that Paul had come at me with a knife, and that I was forced to leave with nothing. She was incensed that I left in the back of a police car. Of course, Paul wasn't going to admit that to her. Janie also expressed concern about Owen and what he had witnessed. She said that she would love to see him after all these years while I was with her. She offered her support in anything she could do and that she could keep her eye on Owen for me when I was back up North.

I was bursting to see Sarah and Owen again. Sarah was working so she couldn't see me until the Sunday. I picked Owen up the next morning. He came lolloping out of the house. He had grown so tall and handsome. I jumped out of the car and hurried over to him to give him a great big hug. He held on to me as if his life depended on it. Me too. I had missed him so much. He pointed and laughed at the eyelashes on my car, "Typical," he chuckled. I giggled too as we got in the car to go to our favourite beach side café for lunch.

Since I had moved back up North, I had seen loads of pictures of Owen on social media with his friends. They seemed to have been taken at the house. It was a bit strange to me that Paul would let him have friends round so often. It didn't look like they were being supervised. I didn't understand why Paul would allow that in his home. When I told Janie about it, she insisted that we investigate. I was really reluctant to go on my own. I didn't want to see Paul but needed to do this. So, Janie offered to come with me. She was sure that if Paul was at the house, he wouldn't kick off if she was with me.

When we arrived at the house, we noticed that there weren't any cars on the drive. Strange. The place looked empty. Eventually, Owen opened the door. He looked terrible, pasty faced and really shocked to see us; especially Janie. He quickly half closed the door. I knew something was wrong. I asked him to let us in. He resisted at first, and then opened the door a little wider. We followed him into the lounge. He sat on the sofa as he cupped his head in his hands; looking embarrassed.

What a bloody mess. The whole place stunk of booze. There were empty cans all over the place, pizza boxes and stuff everywhere. What the hell was going on? I had so many questions and didn't know what to ask him first. So, I asked him where Paul was. Owen wouldn't tell me; he was tearful and looked awkward. It was that loyalty thing again. I told him that I wasn't cross with him, though I needed to know what was going on. After a few minutes of painful silence, he told me that Paul had moved in with a woman six months ago. What? I was livid! I couldn't take it in. I couldn't understand why Paul would fight so much to keep Owen; take him away from me and then neglect him. Owen also admitted that Paul popped back once a week to throw some ready meals in the fridge for Owen, and then retreat back to his girlfriend's house leaving Owen alone.

Owen confessed that he was lonely living on his own. At first it was fun, as this was 'the fun house.' Then his friends began staying over. Word got out that there were no parents around so there were more friends arriving and loads of parties on the weekend. This became the party house. I was so beyond furious with Paul. I couldn't believe that he would be so neglectful. I couldn't believe that he would be so cavalier with Owen's safety and welfare. It felt like he was using Owen as a pawn in this game to get back at me. I asked Owen to ring Paul that minute. He told me that Paul was coming with groceries shortly. I told him that we would wait. We sat down on the sofa. Owen didn't want a confrontation, understandably. I didn't want to make Owen uncomfortable but I had to confront Paul. Janie was horrified; she started to tidy up the house. My son was living in squalor, unsafe and unsanitary conditions and I hadn't a clue about this. Owen had hidden this from me for months. Whenever I asked about Paul, Owen told me that everything was fine. At this point I asked him why he hadn't told me. He said that he didn't want to worry me. He said that he didn't want to cause any trouble either, and that he had been having a blast with his friends to start with. Then clearly it got out of control. To think that Owen was lonely and living like this, broke my heart. I couldn't wait to give Paul a dressing down and rectify the situation.

When Paul walked in the house, he nearly had a heart attack seeing Janie as well as me standing in the lounge. I tore a strip off him, I couldn't help it, I hit the roof. He was speechless. I could tell that he felt guilty, and that he realized he'd really messed up, by the look on his face, and his silence. I was furious and I just couldn't hold back. I told him that I saw the pictures of crazy parties on Owen's social media. I never dreamed that they were taken at his house. Where was he? Why was he allowing these unsupervised teenagers loose in his home. I also told him that he needed to get the place cleaned up and move back in right now. There was no way that Owen should be living alone, either. He was only sixteen. Paul needed to get his priorities right. He was lucky that the house didn't burn down with Owen and his friends in it or any other number of hideous scenarios. This was unthinkable. He should be looking after him, not neglecting him. Paul didn't even try to defend himself. He promised that he would sort it all out and that he would move back home. I told him that it had to be fulltime and it had to be 'tonight' as Owen could not be on his own one more minute. If he couldn't handle this Owen's was coming with me.

It was as if the train was going off the rails and I had managed to get it back on track. I wished it hadn't got to that point. Janie suggested that we all go out for a comfort meal so Owen, Janie and I got in the car and left. As painful as it was to see Owen in this situation, I was grateful that I had caught it in time. I honestly would never have thought that Paul would allow this for Owen. I was reeling. I asked Owen to come back North with me. He told me that his life was in Somerset. He said that he felt much better that I had sorted out the situation, knowing that Paul would be moving back in that night.

I met up with Sarah the next day. I wanted to see Sarah and Owen separately the first time and then hoped to see them both together before I left. So, we met for lunch at a local fish restaurant. Sarah was her usual bouncy self. She was really happy, loved her job, had loads of friends and wouldn't want to be anywhere else.

Thank God. I could rest easily about her. We had real giggles over lunch. Sarah is just so funny. I dropped her back home in time for her to go out with her friend later in the day. She agreed to see me again with Owen the following day. I was looking forward to that and booked a nice restaurant for a gentleman's brunch. We all had a lovely time and it was like the old days, catching up.

After brunch I headed back up North. Owen told me over brunch that Paul was indeed moving his belongings back into the house. It was hard leaving both Sarah and Owen, though I knew I would be back again as soon as I could. Janie promised me that I was welcome any time. I was incredibly lucky to have her as my lovely friend. She promised that she would keep an eye on Owen for me, too.

I felt lonely when I got home. The house was quiet. It was lovely, though it didn't feel cosy to me. I didn't feel like making it my home, either. It felt as if I was staying in a guest house. I couldn't seem to settle. I started to think about looking for a house share. I noticed an advert for a female to share a flat in Hackness. The owner was looking for someone 'mature and easy going.' That was me, I thought. So, I enquired about it by email. Within minutes, I received a response. I arranged to meet the lady. When I arrived, I realized that the flat was on the same street that Donovan had lived on in the B&B years ago. That could be a good or a bad omen.

It was lovely; a spacious third floor flat. There were four floors in the building. Helena, the owner, was a gorgeous girl; petite and probably in her late thirties. We got on well immediately as we walked through the flat and she showed me the room. It was spacious. I loved it; it was inviting and furnished nicely. It reminded me of Jackie's flat. She told me that we would share the kitchen and the bathroom. She also offered for me to use the lounge with her. I felt that this would feel more like home for me than where I was currently living. She had a tubby, lazy ginger cat strolling around too, which was nice.

On the spot I told her that I would like to take it. Later that day, I spoke to Amy and Mike about my decision. I told them that I had found a lovely place and was giving them the proper notice. They were excited for me and I was very grateful to them for everything they had done for me. I spent the next month enjoying my time with Amy and Mike listening to music and socialising with their friends in Mike's whacky garden 'pub.' We really bonded over this time and I knew that I would always have a special place in my heart for both of them.

I moved in with Helena a month later. I felt at home as soon as I moved in. We got on really well. We liked similar things and spent most evenings watching TV together. I felt happy and content. She was a great cook and she liked to experiment on me. I didn't complain about that. While I was on my own, I couldn't be bothered to cook anything, just for myself. I was settling in nicely and feeling more grounded.

I was feeling more myself. I had my quirky, fun car with the lashes, and a lovely place to call home. Most probably this was only temporary but it was just what I needed at this time. I was due to receive my divorce settlement soon. I decided that I could have a rethink when I received the funds. I needed to get a home to call my own. At the moment though, I was taking it one month at a time.

Thankfully, it wasn't long before our divorce came through. It happened to be Valentine's Day 2012. What a relief. Finally, I was free. Part of me was sad because it was an ending. I was hopeful for what would have come next, as well. A couple of months later, I received my settlement. What a massive relief. I was happy to finally be divorced. I felt free to start my life again. Though I had a tinge of sadness for Paul, I was sure that it was the right thing for both of us. It was the best thing for both of us.

I arranged to take the 'girls' out for a posh meal at a local restaurant to celebrate. I took great joy in treating my dear friends and joked that the 'meal was on Paul.' We had a great night. I felt happy to be with my girls. They had shared so much of my life. I wanted to thank them all for standing by me and believing in me. They will never know how much I loved them and still do. They also suggested that I write a book. I chuckled, saying "Seriously, would anyone want to read my crazy story?"

CHAPTER 19

The Life Changing Party - 2012

I spoke to Owen as regularly as you can with a teenager! He confirmed that Paul had moved back in the house, together with his girlfriend, Sherry. Owen said that he didn't get on very well with Sherry, but at least his dad was back with him. Paul bought a large summerhouse for Owen's eighteenth birthday. He erected it in the back garden. Owen was pleased to have his privacy and a place for his friends. Thankfully, he could only fit two of them in at a time! Owen put his Xbox and a sofa in there, so he was happy. He assured me that he slept in the house but used the summerhouse as his 'lounge.' We made plans to see each other very soon.

Tyler and the band were extremely busy. They were in Italy on their European Tour. I stayed connected with him via WhatsApp. Tyler told me that they were working on their first album, and that it was going well. He said that the album would be due for release in a month or so. Wow! I was ecstatic to hear that. He mentioned that they were working on their videos too. Things were really happening and moving fast for Tyler and the boys. Meanwhile, Sarah had started a new office job. She was having an absolute blast, as usual. She was loving life. She had great workmates, they enjoyed loads of banter between them and worked hard. Every time I spoke to Sarah, afterwards, I was happy. She made my heart smile.

I fell into a routine of work during the week, and seeing Amy, Mark, and the girls for lunch most Saturday afternoons. I also visited Mam every weekend. Sometimes, Harry and Dina would come over too. I tried to see Mam after work three of four times a week, as well. Mam was often feeling down when I arrived, but by the time I left, she was giggling. That felt good. We would have a cup of tea and a good natter, mostly about the TV show, *'Strictly Come Dancing,'* or the neighbour's antics. We were growing much closer. I cherished my time with her. Her health was deteriorating, so she didn't get out very much. She would spend most of her time reading. Mam often joked with me about my writing a book. She was amused by my various antics and my American adventure. She felt that my life could be an inspiring story. Mam suggested that it may be cathartic for me to get everything written down, as well. So many people up to now had suggested this but for some reason when Mam suggested it, I thought perhaps she may have a point. It did seem like a way for me to make sense of it all. I did want to find a way of telling my kids the truth about my life. She was really the one that encouraged me over our many chats.

One Saturday afternoon in the month I spent with Amy, Jackie, and Little Eileen. Amy introduced me to Lyla and Petra. Petra worked for Amy, and Lyla was a close friend of Petra's. They were all wonderful girls. I hit it off instantly with all of them and felt part of something special. Lyla was striking, with glossy shoulder length, auburn hair. It reminded me of a horse's mane. She had beautiful, bright blue eyes and a wonderful tan. Petra was slim and blonde with deep brown eyes, and very tanned too. They both looked radiant and the picture of health.

Amy invited me to celebrate Petra's 40th birthday party. It was to be held in their garden 'pub.' I was tired from the week so I really couldn't be bothered to go anywhere. I was trying to decide all afternoon whether to go. Helena tempted me to stay at home. She offered to cook, and we could watch a film. That sounded perfect to me. Just as I was deciding to stay at home, Amy rang to check that I was still coming to the party. She told me that she and Petra were worried that nobody would turn up. The pressure was on. Before I knew it, I had a soak in the bath, fiddled with my hair, threw on some glitzy clothes, and was on my way. I didn't have the heart to say no. I was slightly nervous because I didn't really know Lyla and Petra that well. I decided that I would stay for a couple of hours, and then slip away. I was sure that nobody would notice. I knew that the party would be a success. Parties were always fun in the 'pub.' I was relieved to know that it was just going to be couples and the odd singleton like me. I was certain that this would be a single man free zone, and I liked that. I was quite happy being with my girl friendships and being single, at last. I really felt fine on my own and that I didn't want any more complications. I enjoyed my kids, my work, and my friends. Life was good.

When I arrived, I was surprised that there was hardly anyone there. Thank God I had made the effort to go. I strolled into the 'pub' and Mike greeted me with a small glass of fizz. That was Mike's way of saying 'hello'! We all congregated around the bar, willing more people to arrive. Gradually they came. Most of them were carrying crates of beer. Within an hour, the party was in full swing. I stayed in the corner, admiring the wall of fame, and watching people arrive. Lyla arrived with a fella following behind her. She hurried over to Amy and Petra. I didn't know much about Lyla's personal circumstances, so I assumed that the fella was her boyfriend. They looked extremely at ease with each other. He was a handsome chap and he looked tanned too. The next minute, Amy came hurtling over to me, saying, "Don't look, but that bloke with Lyla is such a nice bloke. You need to get with him!" "What?" I laughed at her and said, "No chance, I am happy being single, thank you. Anyway, isn't he with Lyla?" "No, no no," Amy said, "That's Spencer. He's Lyla's ex-husband. He is such a lovely bloke. They're on really good terms, that's all. Trust me, he is so nice." She explained that Lyla and Spencer had remained good friends. Amy kept saying, "He's such a decent bloke. He'd be perfect for you. I'll get Lyla to introduce you both."

I panicked as I wasn't prepared for this. I didn't think for a minute that Spencer would be interested in me. Within seconds however, Lyla and Spencer were standing in front of me. Spencer was looking as uncomfortable as I felt. He was smiling awkwardly, and slightly cocked his head as if to say, 'We are in trouble now!' Lyla introduced us. We all chatted together. Spencer asked me about Tyler and the band. Amy had told Lyla all about Tyler and his success. Lyla and Spencer had a 12-year-old son, Luke and he was taking drumming lessons. That broke the ice, and we started talking about Tyler and his drumming experience. Spencer was interested in how Tyler's band had become so well-known. He seemed to be fascinated to hear all about it. He joked that he had always wanted to be in a band, but that he decided he would be much better off being a supply chain manager, instead! He was very funny, and I felt immediately at ease with him. Lyla seemed to 'magically disappear' and so did Amy. We were left alone to chat away.

Spencer and I got on famously. He made me laugh so much. He had such a great sense of humour and I lapped it up. I felt so relaxed with Spencer. I felt tremendously comfortable with him. The conversation flowed so easily. We had an absolute blast, laughing and singing along to the music. Sometimes we were dancing, too. He was a really good dancer; he was quite a mover. It was wonderful. Spencer was a breath of fresh air, confident without being arrogant. During the evening, he kept giving me little pecks on the cheek, and he brushed my arm with his finger as he did it. I liked that. It was sensual.

We became oblivious to everyone else in the room. We had slipped into our own little world. We had a fabulous night. I had never felt so relaxed with a man before. I didn't feel self-conscious about my conversation, nor was I nervous around him. Spencer put me at ease completely. He had a lovely kind face and was very handsome, but it was his personality to which I was really drawn. The way we clicked. His looks were a bonus. I had truly never felt like this before. Oh, blimey this could be dangerous!

The next thing we knew it was 5:00 am. Amy and Mike had gone to bed, and most people had gone home. The night flew by. I didn't want our conversations to stop so luckily, he asked me for my phone number. As he climbed into his car, I remember thinking that there was something special about him. I really hoped that I would see him again.

A couple of days later, my phone beeped while I was at work. It was a comical text from Spencer. He was even hilarious over text. I had a huge smile on my face for the rest of the day. Spencer rang me that evening and we talked for a couple of hours. We continued texting funny flirtations throughout the following week. He rang me at 10:00 pm every night.

CHAPTER 20

The Interview

After a week of comical texting and phone calls in the evening, Spencer mentioned that he wanted to ask me a few questions before he could take our relationship further. At first, I thought he was joking because he was usually so funny. Now he was all very businesslike. He explained that he had two kids and wanted me to be clear about his parenting priorities. He told me that he had arranged for Luke to come to his house the following weekend, but he may be able to see me on that Saturday night as Luke was staying with a friend in Leathley. I was looking forward to seeing Spencer then.

I was nervous most of that Saturday. I didn't really know what to expect. Helena had gone out, so I was alone waiting for Spencer to arrive, which he did about 8:00 pm. When he came into the flat, I noticed that he seemed edgy and nervous. That made me on edge, too. I sensed that he was different to the texting Spencer and the bloke I had met a few days before. He was carrying a pen and notepad. Whoa! I thought this was a bit formal. I didn't want a bloody mortgage or double glazing! As I attempted to lighten the atmosphere, I pointed to the notepad and asked him if I was going to be interviewed. Perhaps was he was writing an article on dating? He remained serious and told me that he had a few questions that he wanted to clarify before we could take things any further. Crickey, I felt like I was under the spotlight!

We sat at the kitchen table. Spencer explained that he had certain arrangements in place with his kids. He was adamant that these arrangements shouldn't be changed. He stressed that it was vital that they must come first; especially with Luke. Spencer was very particular about him. I didn't have a problem with this at all. It suited me to have weekends to myself. I was in no hurry to change that. I certainly wasn't ready to rush into anything too serious, either. I considered that this would work well for both of us. Spencer was insistent that he would continue to have Luke two weekends in a row, and then take one off, on a three-week cycle. I could understand why that would put some people off, but it didn't bother me at all. In fact I respected his commitment.

Spencer's arrangement with Chantelle was different as she was only five. It was very much driven by her mother. Chantelle didn't sleep overnight. He usually saw her after nursery school during the week for a couple of hours and at the weekends when her mother allowed. This meant that he enjoyed time with Luke but had plenty of time with them both together, too. As the 'interview' progressed Spencer ticked each point. He presented scenarios and asked me what I would do in certain circumstances. It was all intensely serious, but I found it quite endearing. As the 'interview' progressed, I poured each of us a glass of wine, and we both relaxed a bit. Spencer remained serious until he had finished his 'questionnaire'! After all of the questions, scenarios, and box ticking were complete, I hoped that I had passed the test. Actually, I found it all quite endearing and hot. I really respected and admired the clarity and care he showed toward his kids. What a great dad! Honestly having clear boundaries, expectations discussed and how we would be together was a first for me. I was seeing that parents really can be kind, respectful, loving, and real. Spencer was showing me this. This was a huge step up for me and this was where I wanted to be. I was beginning to feel worthy of this.

Spencer knew most of my story by now, particularly the consequences of my divorce and the ups and downs journey with my children. I reassured him that I absolutely understood how painful it is to be separated from our kids. I told him that I would never interfere with his arrangements. I would be more than happy to fit in with him and their routine. It suited me to have my own time and space as well, so we were on to a winner as far as I was concerned.

I was still healing, learning to trust, and finding myself after my American adventure. I hoped that my growth and being in Spencer's life with Luke and Chantelle would allow me to share my love when they came over.

Spencer stayed with me that night. We spent most of the night cuddling, giggling, and chatting. It was lovely. We talked for ages, while we cuddled. We discovered that we had so much in common. The next morning, Spencer left early. He wanted to spend some time with Luke. I felt so happy and content when he left. There was a small part of me that wondered if this was all 'too good to be true.'

I didn't doubt that Spencer would call me. He did indeed at 8:00 pm that night. We had a lovely romantic chat and in the middle of it he said, "You are no longer single." I was delighted to hear that, and I told him that he wasn't either! I finally met my soulmate, and I knew it. With others there was always an element of doubt. With Spencer I felt sure. Then he said, "Let's go away on Saturday for an overnight." How exciting! I asked him for details, but he wanted to surprise me. We arranged to meet the following Saturday afternoon.

I was so giddy when we met that day. When I drove up, I flashed my eyelash covered lights at him. He stepped out of his car and strolled towards me. He pointed at the diamante jeweled eyelashes on my car! He was speechless then he did manage to raise a reserved giggle. With a quick peck on my cheek, we set off in convoy to his place. I was excited to see what his house was like. When we arrived at his house, I was bursting to find out where we were going. He announced that we were off to Nottingham! So we weren't going to Paris! I didn't want to fly anyway. He explained that we were going to a 40th birthday party, hosted by his best friend, Niall. It was for Raquel, Naill's fiancé. What absolute fun! I was slightly concerned that it may be a bit soon to be meeting Spencer's best friend let alone his other friends, but I was certain that they would all be lovely. Spencer assured me that I would really enjoy them, and that I would fit in perfectly.

We had such a laugh that night. I soon relaxed and enjoyed myself. We were up dancing until the early hours. We stayed overnight at their gorgeous house. Everyone made me feel welcome. I had a feeling that we were all going to become firm friends. What a relief. Spencer and I were so happy together. Everyone seemed genuinely pleased to meet me, and were happy for Spencer, too.

I understood why Niall and Raquel were so important to Spencer. They had been great friends to Spencer and had supported him through his challenging relationships in the past. I liked them both very much. They were quite the 'power couple.' Raquel was a criminal law solicitor. She was so interesting to talk to. She had an incredibly calm presence and a firm, but caring nature. Niall was a director of a large company; doing very well. He was a loveable, cheeky, and hilariously funny character.

Spencer made it clear during the 'interview' that he wouldn't rush to introduce me to his kids. He wanted to be sure about both of our feelings beforehand. When we arrived back to Leathley the next day, Spencer had arranged to spend the afternoon with Chantelle. I was nervously delighted when Spencer asked me to stay and meet her.

Chantelle came bursting through the door like a whirlwind. She immediately started chattering and didn't stop. She breezed past me, oblivious to my being there. We couldn't get a word in edgeways. She was a little firecracker. She was a sweetheart and super cute, too. Without even being introduced we flopped on the floor together and started playing with her little dolls in her wooden dollhouse. We were rearranging the furniture in the rooms and changing the tiny clothes on the dolls. Spencer was sitting on the sofa, watching, and enjoying us. After we enjoyed our afternoon tea, Spencer prepared to take Chantelle home. I was preparing to leave too when Spencer asked me to stay. He said that he would be back in half an hour. So I stayed.

We got up early the next morning, Spencer

made coffee then I made it back to Hackness, just in time for work. Spencer and I couldn't bear being apart. I went to see him most nights after work. Sometimes I would pick up some Italian food at the local market, or Spencer would cook, while I perched on a stool at the breakfast bar gazing at him. We talked about everything and laughed our way through our meals. I had never felt so comfortable with anyone before. Not like this. I felt that our time together was special. We had become such good friends very quickly, and of course lovers, too. Everything seemed natural to us both.

As the days and weeks went by, we began to grow even closer. If I were enjoying time at my place, Spencer would call me those evenings at 10:00 pm. We would talk for ages; having deep and soulful conversations. I felt that I could trust him and that he would always be there for me. For the first time in years, I slept well knowing that I had someone special in my life who had honorable values; a man of integrity and strength. Someone I was proud to be with.

I began to stay with Spencer when he wasn't being an awesome dad with his kids. We either spent it in Leathley together, or we would go to Nottingham to spend time with Niall and Raquel. Sometimes we would go to Hackness to see Amy and Mike, too. I looked forward to our weekends together, but still enjoyed my alone time.

Halloween was looming. Spencer suggested that it would be an ideal time for me to meet Luke. Spencer was protective about their relationship. When Spencer told Luke about me, he had shown signs of doubt. I agreed to come to Spencer's after work. I suggested that we take Luke and Chantelle out Trick or Treating. I thought that this would be a fun ice breaker. I bought a huge witch's hat, a cloak, and oversized eyelashes to match my car. I got face paints and vampire teeth, really scary masks, cobwebs, decorations for the house and a couple of little buckets for their treats. I included Spencer, with a vampire outfit and a terrifying mask. I wore a witch's cape, oversized witches velvet hat, and carried a magic wand that lit up.

I knocked on the door and they invited me in. Luke came straight over to me. He was so cute, and polite. He held out his hand for us to shake hands. I knew instantly that we were going to get along. Luke immediately allowed me to start the Halloween transformation, and within minutes he was a vampire. Soon after that there was another knock at the door. Chantelle arrived. Of course she was in a designer mini 'Wicked' witch costume, complete with black fishnet gloves and little black shiny boots. She had a custom-made twig broom. She looked amazing. We zoomed around the streets darting from house to house. It was such fun and I loved being part of it.

It was half term, so Luke was staying until Sunday night. I left early the next morning as it was Friday and I needed to go to work. We arranged for me to spend my first Saturday night with Spencer and Luke. Luke and I got on so well; we immediately clicked. He was such a lovely boy, and very polite. I was about to leave for work when Luke gave me a massive hug. As Spencer walked me out, I noticed tears in his eyes as he said that Luke had never hugged any of his other girlfriends. I was thrilled.

When I arrived on Saturday, Spencer and Luke were doing Luke's homework at the kitchen table. I soon settled in, made myself at home as I curled up on the couch with a magazine. I occupied myself until they had finished. In the afternoon we played games on the Wii. Spencer cooked a lovely dinner, and we snuggled down to watch a film. We had a very relaxed time together; it all seemed so natural. We enjoyed spending time together.

Spencer took Luke home on Sunday afternoon and I stayed to enjoy Sunday evening with him. He shared with me how he normally hated Sunday evenings after having the kids. He appreciated me being there for that emotional transition. He was thrilled that we had all got along over the weekend. It was a breakthrough for us.

I left early that Monday morning. I had only got halfway home, when I realized that I had left my handbag at Spencer's house. I pulled over and rang Spencer, straightaway. Without hesitation, he suggested that I wait there, and that he would bring my bag to me. Nothing was too much trouble for Spencer; he was really kind. As he pulled up behind my car, I looked in my mirror and watched him get out of the car carrying my bag. That was the light bulb moment when I knew that I had fallen in love with him. It was an overwhelming feeling which I had never felt before. This must be love. Something told me that I was falling, and there was nothing I could do. I didn't want to be without him. The feeling scared me, but I knew damn well that I loved him and hoped that he loved me.

That night I went back to Spencer's. He told me that he had something to show me in the bedroom. When we went into the bedroom, he ushered me towards the bedside table on 'my side' of the bed, then he pulled out the top drawer. I noticed that it was empty. Spencer proudly announced that this was to become 'my drawer'! I giggled and thought it was the sweetest gesture. I knew this was his attempt to make me feel at home.

I was keen for Spencer to meet Sarah and Owen, so we arranged a trip to Somerset. It was November so the weather wasn't brilliant, but I wanted to see them both before Christmas. Spencer booked a lovely hotel opposite the beach. I used to dream about staying there when I lived in Minehead, so this was a real treat for me. Those days when I would run past that hotel came flooding back to me.

As soon as Spencer met Sarah, they hit it off. Spencer went straight up to her, gave her a hug, and kissed her on the cheek saying, "Hello Sarah, I'm Spencer and your mum has told me so many lovely things about you." Sarah replied, "Okay, so I will be calling you Spence." We all laughed, and the ice was broken. Owen was more reserved at first; being quiet and subdued. I could tell that Owen approved of Spencer. He clearly was impressed that I had finally met a respectable bloke. As we enjoyed our dinner together, we had a wonderful time. Sarah forever being the funny one said, "This person is a real man." Owen told me that he felt Spencer seemed very solid, self-assured, and sound. They noticed how intelligent, generous, and gracious he was to all of us as well as the waiting staff. They noticed how respectful and honouring he was to me. They really enjoyed his company, his good manners, and his kindness. They definitely enjoyed his humour. Sarah and Spencer bantered hilariously all through dinner. What a relief. Through their eyes I could really see what I had in Spencer.

The next day even though Sarah so enjoyed our time together, she had made previous plans so she couldn't join us. So Owen, Spencer and I went off to the go-karting track nearby. They hopped in their go-karts, strapped on their helmets, and raced off. It was so fun being a spectator as they whizzed by me. When they finished and took their helmets off, they were laughing and high fiving all the way over to me. We walked over to the post-race room. We looked up at the score board and of the ten drivers, Owen had won!

We had a lovely couple of days, which were over too soon as we were heading back North. The time together was a complete success. The most important thing to me was for all of us to connect and we certainly did. Spencer was able to keep everything positive. He found ways to connect with both of my kids. Sarah with their humour, intelligence, and hospitality world. Owen with his love of everything to do with cars. My kids noticed how loving he was when he spoke about his kids. They could tell he was a really good dad. They were simply impressed with Spencer and happy for me.

A few days before Christmas, Helena asked me whether I intended to move in with Spencer as I was hardly ever at the flat. She had noticed that Spencer and I were getting closer. I told her that I didn't intend to move in just yet, but if Spencer asked me to, I would consider it. She was very understanding and wanted me to be happy. She asked me to let her know as soon as I had decided, so that she could advertise my room.

Spencer and I began edging around the situation. One morning, I was about to leave for work. We were saying goodbye in the hallway. I turned to kiss him, when suddenly, he told me that he loved me. I shuddered with delight from top to toe. I realized that he meant it and that he had said it first! I refrained from saying it back. Spencer then invited me to bring more of my belongings over. I paused and took a second for myself. That's when Spencer asked me to share his home with him. At that moment I realized that I had reached another crossroads in my life. This time I was really able to chose and not just consider the demands of others. The difference this time was that I could feel in my heart that this choice was truly best for me. I was choosing Spencer.

I was ecstatic. I cried all the way back to Hackness. I felt euphoric. Finally, true love had found me, and his name was Spencer. It felt incredible. What a feeling! This Christmas was different to any I had spent in a long time. We dressed the tree together with Spencer's ornaments. While we played constant Christmas music, we wrapped gifts for our kids and did all the other traditional things including eating way too much chocolate! Luke had Christmas Day with Lyla and his stepsister Yolanda so then he came to us on Boxing Day. We spent an incredibly fun New Year's Eve with Amy and Mike in the 'pub.' We planned activities for the

New Year and made hopeful resolutions. Of course this year we hoped we would keep them.

We popped in to see Mam most weekends, after we had dropped Luke home. I used to spend time with Mam on Saturday afternoons too. Spencer played tennis with Luke then, so I had plenty of time to chat with her. I loved spending time with Mam, we shared the same humor, and spent the afternoons supping tea and giggling about telly programs and suchlike. I especially appreciated the deep chats that we had. At this time in my life as I realized the importance and necessity of truly finding myself, I needed my Mam. She never judged me. I knew I was always going to be safe with her. Everything we talked about we would keep between ourselves. She allowed me to work through my inner entanglement. I knew she loved me, wanted the best for me and understood that I did need to find a way to finding myself. I will always appreciate that time with Mam as she shared her insight about me as only a mam can do. Through this time with her she enabled me to take a good look at myself. To this day those conversations are my guiding lights. Mam was very relieved that Spencer and I had met. She felt that he was a good man. She told me that he was exactly what she wished for me. Mam recognized my growth and belief in myself to allow such a healthy relationship.

CHAPTER 21

Happily Ever After? – 2013

The following Autumn Spencer and I flew to Porto and then Madeira for a ten day holiday. We spent lovely days lazing on the sand and enjoying the fabulous local dishes in the harbourside restaurants in the evenings. It was so romantic; we fell in love with Porto and more with each other. We were next to a fabulous beach bar, enjoying the sun and the wonderful music that wafted from the restaurants and bars along the beach. We talked nonstop; discussing the future. We flew on to Madeira and stayed in a beautiful hotel in the town centre. It had wonderful gardens and we spent a couple of days sightseeing the local area.

When we got back home, we had another day off before the weekend. We were sitting in the kitchen having breakfast. Spencer looked at me and said, "We might as well go into Leathley and look for a ring." I couldn't believe it. I was ecstatic! "Are you joking"? I asked. "I couldn't be more serious," Spencer said. I whizzed upstairs to get ready which I did in record time. We drove into Leathley with huge smiles on our faces. I was so excited.

We browsed around some jeweller's shops; we didn't find anything that we liked. I didn't want to get something just for the sake of it and I knew I didn't want a traditional engagement ring, either. Then, we found it. As soon as I tried it on, I knew that this one was the one for me. I immediately burst into tears. Spencer teared up and asked the shop assistant to 'box it up'. She handed the posh bag with the ribbon on it to him. Oh my God. This was real. As we walked out of the shop, he told me that he wanted to propose properly.

We drove towards Hackness, stopping at a pub with a huge beer garden at the back and green fields filled with sheep surrounding it. He gently took hold of my hand and led me over to the fountain surrounded by cobble stones. This was a serious moment. Spencer looked into my eyes and said, "I would be honoured if you would be my wife." We both filled with tears again. I said, "Yes, of course." We hugged and danced to our own music. I hadn't felt that level of happiness; maybe ever. What a fabulous feeling!

Spencer slipped the ring on my finger and, that was it. We were engaged. That ring was never coming off! Spencer had bought a ring for himself, too. He wanted something on his finger to show that we were officially engaged now. We were incredibly happy. Both of us couldn't stop smiling. The first place we went to announce our engagement was to Mam's. She was her usual calm self on the outside but I knew she was pleased. She smiled and said that she was happy for us. She took my hand and gave me a knowing and loving squeeze.

Next, we zoomed up to Spencer's parents' house to give them the good news. They were really overjoyed for us and opened a bottle of bubbles to celebrate. We each wanted to tell our kids face to face so we shared the happy news with them the next time we saw each of them. They were all delighted and Chantelle immediately asked if she could be a bridesmaid.

We decided not to rush into the wedding. We both wanted to get it right and take our time with the arrangements. When I lived in Hackness with Donovan I used to go to a beautiful and grand church in the centre of the town. I loved going there. When I needed time alone, I would go and sit in this two hundred year old church. When I walked in the door, every time I felt peace, calm, and warmth. It was always so beautifully lit with the sun streaming through the stain glass, reflecting colours all around the sanctuary. I could just sit with my thoughts and my feelings with no-one would bother me. The vicar was there and had all the time in the world for me if I needed guidance. If not, he left me alone. I've never felt anywhere else such a feeling of safety, happiness, and joy. So, I felt strongly that I wanted to start my married life with Spencer in this house of love. I always thought that it would be lovely to get married there though, I never dreamed that it may actually happen. Spencer shared my same sentiments and so together we made it happen.

Next on the wedding journey was to start looking around for a dress. I didn't know what I wanted, but I knew I wanted to have fun looking. It was going to be during the summer so that would influence my choice. I looked at all styles; fitted, off the shoulder, mermaid style, sleek and silky. What I did want was something in cream and a jewelled bodice. Often, I went on my own as I preferred to do so. But this one day, I invited Amy to join me. As soon as I tried this particular dress on, I knew it was the one. When I stepped out of the fitting room Amy's eyes filled with tears and she simply nodded, 'Yes.' It was indeed a cream fitted bodice with jewels. From the bodice flowed a deliciously full length with subtle netting and a beautiful train. It was full of sparkle, just like me. I felt amazing in it. I had come alive again. I couldn't have been happier.

Amy was to be my matron of honour. I would also have three bridesmaids, Sarah, Chantelle, and Yolanda; Chantelle and Luke's half-sister. Owen and Luke were to be the groomsmen. Niall was going to be Spencer's Best Man. Of course, who else? We booked the Golf Club in Hackness for the reception and we were crazy busy making the arrangements. It was fun, even though it was stressful. The plans kept getting bigger.

Spencer and I didn't want a big wedding at first. We were leaning to something more intimate. We ended up with about a hundred and fifty people on the guest list, a swing band, a magician, and a swanky wedding car. So much for small weddings! I was feeling wonderful about it all. I was absolutely thrilled when Tyler agreed to give me away, as long as he was back from his world tour. He would make sure that he was.

As Mam was becoming more immobile, she started making noises about not coming to the wedding. I was really disappointed at the thought of her not coming to my big day. It wouldn't have been the same without her there. She had always been such an important part of my life and I couldn't imagine her not being part of this. I wanted her to witness this powerful and positive next step in my life. Mam's blessing was so important to me. Knowing she was there with me would mean the world to me.

My childhood and many years after that were filled with memories of Mam in her church life. She so enjoyed the comfort of the church community. She was very involved and went to church often. She was even the president of the Mother's Union for two years. I wasn't able to create this sacred ceremony with my previous marriages so part of my wish was to give Mam this sacred day. I also loved her and I wanted her to be proud of me.

Spencer had a stag do; a weekend at the coast with a handful of his mates. Niall was in charge, naturally. His best friend from down south travelled up. They went cycling, or at least they tried to, in the afternoon. I think they found that too much like hard work and gave up after an hour or so. They ended up going out to a few pubs and for a meal later on. It was pretty low key and just how Spencer wanted it to be.

My hen party took place on a river cruise. There were about twenty-five of us altogether. It was hilarious; we had a blast. We met in Hackness and all took the bus to the dock. There were three other hen parties on the cruise; no men in sight apart from the driver. We had a tasty dinner buffet with a disco for dancing on board. We sang, danced, and chatted while we cruised up and down the river. It was perfect. Everyone had a wonderful time, waving at the people sitting outside the pubs along the way. It was a night to remember. I couldn't believe that all the girls had made it. Everyone was in great spirits and genuinely happy for me. It was such a good night. We all enjoyed it so much that we vowed to do it again every year, here's hoping for next year!

We had the rehearsal for the wedding at the church on the Thursday night before the big day. Tyler made it to the church in the nick of time and Sarah had driven up with Owen that day. It was really lovely to have them all with me. The last time that had happened was at my 50th birthday celebration in Minehead. So much had happened since then. I loved seeing them together with all their banter, laughter, and the love. It made my heart burst with pride.

Tyler was staying in a hotel near the church. Spencer booked rooms for Sarah, Owen, and me for the night before the wedding as well as one for himself. We hosted a meal at a local Italian restaurant the night before where we invited friends and family. They were all staying at a hotel nearby. We included Mam too but she wanted to save her strength for the big day. Another great night with food, frivolity, and great conversation.

After the meal, Spencer walked me back to the hotel and we said, "good night" at the hotel front revolving doors. He kissed me on the cheek, gave me a gentle hug and wished me 'sweet dreams.' He started to walk away and then turned back to me and said, "See you at the church."

I was sharing a room with Sarah. We talked for ages and had a proper giggle that night as sleep was not going to happen. She loved 'Spence' as she called him. She had no doubt that we were doing the right thing. We suited each other so well. Of course, ever being the humorous Sarah, she told me not to mess it up this time!

The morning of the wedding I awoke with

butterflies and started getting ready with Sarah. Amy turned up around 11:00 am to collect us. She chauffeured us over to her home as we had arranged for the bride's party to leave for the church from Mike's garden 'pub' where Spencer and I had first met. I continued getting ready with all the girls in the wedding party while the photographer snapped photos. The photographer managed to get great shots of Chantelle and Yolanda as they ran around the garden in their bridesmaid dresses. He got lots of candid shots of us getting our hair and makeup done. He even managed to get a few great shots of me. We had a few posed shots in the garden, as well. I was extremely excited though I was getting nervous too. I couldn't believe that we were actually getting married 'today.' I couldn't wait.

Tyler turned up at Amy's house to join us. He looked amazing in his navy suit. The wedding car came for all of us and whisked us to the church on time. As we drove over, I was now really nervous. Tyler quietly told me to relax and that everyone was happy for me. This was a joyful day. We pulled up to the front of the church. We all climbed out and posed as more photos were taken, then we went into the church. The vicar was a female who was the spit of the *'Vicar of Dibley'*. That put me at ease. I couldn't help it. I chuckled when I saw her in her gear. She was lovely. Really fun, too.

We had arranged for one of the songs from Tyler's band's album for our walk down the aisle. Sarah, Amy, and the girls had gone down the aisle before me. When I peeped through the curtain to look at them, I caught a glimpse of Spencer standing next to Niall. My husband to be looked amazing, handsome, and calm. He looked incredibly happy. Thank God for that. I wanted to run down the aisle to him.

Walking down the aisle holding hands with my son Tyler, to Tyler's music, toward my new husband was overwhelmingly joyful and amazing. More than my dreams had come true. The grand church with its sky high ceilings and sacred history all around looked stunning. The scent of the lilies and incense filled the church. It was a true good omen that the sun was shining that day and through the stained glass windows reflecting colours all around. It was as if a magical peace was surrounding all of us. As Tyler and I walked down the aisle, I felt all the love from my family and friends. Especially, from Mam who was proudly sitting in the front row next to Harry in her beautiful Sunday best. As I approached the alter, I caught her eye and we smiled at each other.

Little Eileen, Carol, Luke, Chantelle, and Yolanda, all read touching poems. The vicar did a beautiful job with her blessings and officiating the ceremony. Spencer and I were so moved and touched by all of this. Then came the time for our vows to each other. As we spoke our love, the room was silent around us. We truly were now merging into one. I honestly felt it. Then the hymns were sung and classical music filled the air while we signed the register. We celebrated our way down the aisle and out of the church for more photographs. We were on a high; over the moon. We had done it. We were now married.

The reception was being held quite nearby, so we didn't have too long before we were in front of everyone again. Everything went smoothly. God knows that was a miracle. Niall's speech will go down in history; it was bang on. He was hilarious! Everyone was roaring with laughter. He lapped it up; well deserved. We all raised a glass in memory of my Dad. I wanted him to be part of my very special day too. Spencer and I were immensely touched.

Everyone had a blast. The party went on until midnight. Sarah was her usual charming self as she darted around, calling Spencer 'Dad.' He loved it. She added so much life and soul to the party. It was good to see all of our five kids together having a great time. That was another dream of mine; to have them all happily in the same room. Complete. Owen was chatting with people and making sure all the guests were happy. It was so great to see Tyler and Owen having their own private chats throughout the evening, too. Dina, Harry, and Mam all enjoyed the reception together. I had a lovely moment with each of them as they shared their love and joy for me. The reception was everything I wished for.

Spencer had booked a charming country hotel for the wedding night, where we arrived just after midnight. He had to use a fork to get all the buttons undone from the back of my dress. What a laugh we had as we were fiddling around with the dress for ages. We fell into bed after that performance. We were exhausted yet content and happy.

The next morning, we had breakfast in our room celebrating our first morning as man and wife. We both felt elated. We were going back home for one night only, as we were flying somewhere for our honeymoon on the Sunday. The destination was yet another secret to me. Sarah and Owen set off earlier that morning to return to Somerset. Tyler had gone on an early train back to the band. Niall and Raquel came to the hotel to say goodbye before we checked out. We drove to see Mam before going to Leathley to get ready for the honeymoon. She was a bit worn out from the celebrations but she was thrilled to have been part of our big day. She was also honoured to be among the first to see us as man and wife. That night we opened all of our generous wedding gifts. What a great feeling. Finally, I had found and married the man of my dreams. My friend, my love, and soulmate.

Sunday morning, we were up early to catch our flight. I was filled with anticipation as I didn't know where we were going. Spencer was ever the gentleman to let me know at least the climate for my honeymoon wardrobe. Spencer told me that he would reveal to me our destination when were arrived at the airport. Luckily, we made it to the airport in the nick of time, rushing through to Departures with only minutes to spare.

We boarded the plane to Malta.

This was the beginning of our new life together.

Thank you, God. I had survived.

EPILOGUE

Well done and thank you for managing to go through all of this with me. I'm sitting in a café enjoying my cup of afternoon tea. I'm at a window seat and it's raining outside. As I sit here, I feel that there is a bit left to say to you. I feel as if I am speaking to a dear friend. I really want you to know my heart. I want you to know who I am from here looking back at all of my journey.

The first thing I want to share with you is why I actually wrote this book. Honestly, if I had known how painful a writing journey this would be, I may not have boarded the train. I am grateful that I was brave enough to pick up my pen and to be totally honest, raw, and candid with myself. At times I honestly felt humiliated, ashamed, and scared to expose so much of my inner emotions and thoughts with you.

When I started this book, I hadn't actually done the excavation to understand the "why" of my choices. I just lived with a general sense of sadness and self-judgement of my past and the consequences. Now I can feel the compassion for who I was along the way. I may not always appreciate my choices but the "why" I now understand. I didn't always have the strength, self-love, and clarity. I didn't always see a good path before me. I didn't always know that I had the power to 'find my way through' in a safe and healthy way. I often felt that 'I had no choice,' that I was a victim of circumstances and that I may not actually 'make it.' I always hoped that my choices for my kids would turn out to be the best for them. Somehow, they were able to navigate all the challenges in their lives and have become truly unique and amazing human beings.

So, my friend from here I can say that I have learned so very much. I have learned after all of this that I did have the strength, I am worth it and I have got the power to carry on. I have found my inner self and the person I have always been but couldn't see. By clearing some of the guilt and shame, I now have more space for love, peace, and kindness not only to others but to myself as well. Through all of this, most of all I have learned that I am enough and my heart is still intact. My heart and soul will always live on through Tyler, Sarah, Owen and now Spencer, Luke, and Chantelle. God willing of course, in the little ones to come; just as we do from our beloved parents. So, my friend this is my cautionary tale and humble story. It has made me who I am today; with all my ditzy, glitzy, whacky, and wonderful qualities. Through all of this journey I am definitely wiser. Mam's wish was that my story would inspire at least one person. I wish for that as well. Hopefully, that's you.

   Love,
       Ruth

www.ingramcontent.com/pod-product-compliance
Lightning Source LLC
Chambersburg PA
CBHW071603080526
44588CB00010B/1005